Everybody Has a Guardian Angel

Everybody Has a Guardian Angel

*And Other Lasting Lessons
I Learned in Catholic Schools*

Mitch Finley

CROSSROAD • NEW YORK

1995

The Crossroad Publishing Company
370 Lexington Avenue, New York, NY 10017

Copyright © 1993 by Mitch Finley

Printed in the United States of America

All quotations from scripture are from the New Revised Standard Version
Bible, Copyright 1989, Division of Christian Education of the National
Council of the Churches of Christ in the United States of America.

Library of Congress Cataloging-in-Publication Data

Finley, Mitch.
    Everybody has a guardian angel : —and other lasting lessons I
learned in Catholic school / Mitch Finley.
        p.   cm.
    ISBN 0-8245-1268-5; 0-8245-1393-2 (pbk.)
    1. Catholic Church—Doctrines—Popular works.   2. Catholic
schools—United States.   3. Finley, Mitch.   I. Title.
BX1754.F54   1993
282'.73'09045-dc20
                                                                92-39443
                                                                    CIP

Dedication

This book is for all the teachers and classmates who made my Catholic school experiences so important to me at: Saints Peter and Paul School, Grangeville, Idaho; Saint Patrick's School and DeSales High School, Walla Walla, Washington; Santa Clara University, Santa Clara, California; and Marquette University, Milwaukee, Wisconsin. And in particular, these teachers: Sister Angelica, O.S.B. (wherever she may be), Sister Glenrose Dalrymple, S.P., Sister Rose Estelle, S.P., Sister Dorothy Byrne, S.P., Sister Mildred Marie, S.P., Ms. Kathleen Cronin, Sister Maryann Benoit, S.P., Mr. Jerry Anhorn, Mr. Bill Gray, Dr. Kenneth Eberhard, Dr. Joseph Grassi, Dr. Theodore Mackin, Rev. Austen Fagothey, S.J. (R.I.P.), Dr. Noel Lazure, Dr. J. Coert Rylaarsdam, and Reverend William Kelly, S.J. In particular, these classmates (in the case of women, I use the names I knew them by, since I have no idea what their married names may be): Larry Grewing (wherever he may be), Jerry Nash, Jim Hill, Jim Hansen, Patrick O'Brien, Kathy Hill, Sister Helen Mason, S.P., Sandra Hertel, and Mary Bergevin.

Contents

Introduction

Catholic Schools and Me

On a bright, hot, late August morning in 1953, my mother, my sister, and I walked through the front doors of Saints Peter and Paul School, in Grangeville, Idaho. Grangeville was—still is, for that matter—a lively little burg in north-central Idaho. The red brick school building was only a few years old, and I was impressed by the neatness of the place—new, highly waxed tile floors, new walls, new, gleaming white drinking fountains, new Formica-topped desks lined up in rows in the classrooms where long, deeply green chalkboards hung on the walls.

The principal, a wisp of a Benedictine nun whose name escapes me nearly forty years later, greeted us warmly. I remember noticing how clean she smelled—her black habit with the big white bib-like appurtenance that covered nearly half of the front of her diminutive self. When Sister eyed me kindly from behind rimless glasses and asked my name and age, my mother prompted me to end my replies with, "Sister." "Yes, Sister." "No, Sister." Later, in the rush of everyday, this became, "Yes, S'ter," and "No, S'ter."

I entered third grade that year, and it soon became evident that a Catholic school would be different from the government school I attended for first and second grades. In a Catholic school, we stood whenever an adult entered the room. We began and concluded each school day with prayers: the Our Father, the Hail Mary, the Glory Be. Religious art—of dubious quality, it's true—decorated the walls, as well as the usual letters of the alphabet tumbling along the wall above the chalkboard.

Often, during quiet study periods, a student would approach Sister's desk, whack her little dome-shaped bell, and lead the class in a brief prayer, such as, "My Jesus, mercy," or "Most Sacred Heart of Jesus, have mercy on us." In our innocence, students and teachers alike called these prayers "ejaculations." The idea was to remind us of God's constant loving presence and to nourish a prayerful environment.

Centrally located just above the front chalkboard in our classroom hung a small, simple but realistic crucifix, while a miniature forty-eight star flag protruded from one corner. We recited the Pledge of Allegiance each morning, right along with the Morning Offering, the Our Father, and three Hail Marys.

A couple of years later, our family moved to a small eastern Oregon town, then, a few months later, to an even smaller town in northeastern Oregon. Neither place had a Catholic school, so I spent the second half of the fifth grade and sixth and seventh grades in government schools where I was not happy. Then we moved again, and following eighth grade at Saint Patrick's School, in Walla Walla, Washington, I spent all four years at DeSales High School, named for the patron saint of the Catholic Press. This was quite a coincidence, since years later writing for the Catholic Press would become a big part of my life.

I was not an outstanding student in high school. Also, during my sophomore year my parents separated, later to divorce. In the Catholic climate of the time, the early 1960s, I felt deeply ashamed of this and never talked about it. I even concocted stories for my friends to explain my father's absence. What gave my life stability was the Catholic school I attended. There I had friends, teachers who accepted me, and a constant sense that life had meaning.

What DeSales High School gave me was what a later era would call "a sense of community." There I felt that I belonged. The Sisters of Charity of Providence—they later simplified their name to Sisters of Providence—who staffed the school gave its environment a religious quality. Whether the subject was algebra (at which I failed to shine), biology, religion, or history, the context was one of faith. The Sisters, and the few lay teachers on the staff, cultivated a Catholic culture, one that spoke daily to us of life's ultimate purpose, which was to love God and show loving care for our neighbor.

In retrospect, I can see that at the time DeSales High School was no great shakes academically. Today, it is a combination junior-senior high school, and is much improved. Still, for me DeSales served a higher purpose. It helped me to see that life was worth living by putting me in the company of people who cared about me.

Later, after four years in the U.S. Navy, I enrolled in a Catholic institution of higher learning, Santa Clara University, in California. A Jesuit university, Santa Clara offered, and still offers today, a first-rate college education. As a Religious Studies major, I joined some of the earliest lay students who chose that major in the wake of the post–Vatican II renewal that spun the church around in the late '60s and early '70s. I enjoyed most of my other classes, too, but studying theology in those years was an exhilarating experience.

Plowing through the intellectually taxing works of the great Jesuit theologian Karl Rahner had a profound impact on my understanding of faith, the Church, and the purpose of my own life. We read Joseph Campbell twenty years before he became the darling of Americans in search of a story to live by. I was intellectually inebriated by the books and faith of the enormously talented American Catholic scripture scholar, Father Raymond Brown, and by the thought of the great Protestant theologian Paul Tillich.

In college, I deepened my understanding, and love for, my Catholic faith and for the place of a Catholic culture in my life. Later, in pursuit of a master's degree in Theology at Marquette University, in Milwaukee, Wisconsin, I continued this process in more depth, giving my theological understanding more precision and a broader scope. For me, my studies expressed Saint Anselm's famous description of theology as "faith in search of understanding." At the same time, it was for me "faith in search of adventures."

With the exception of four-and-a-half of my years in elementary school, all of my schooling took place in Catholic institutions. While I cannot say that I was the brightest light to ever walk the halls of the Catholic schools I attended, I can, and do, number myself among those who think back on Catholic schooling with tremendous gratitude. Because of this, my three sons attend Catholic schools, as well.

It is the purpose of this book to share with you, the reader, some of the fundamental lessons I, and countless other Catholics of my generation, learned in Catholic schools. I do not propose a mere exercise in nostalgia. Rather, I would share with you, the reader, how the basic lessons I learned in Catholic schools took root, then grew and developed over the years; how, while clinging to the same truths I learned as a child, I left behind the things of a child in order to embrace ideals and perspectives more appropriate to adult faith.

One of my heroes, Pope John XXIII, said it extremely well. He declared that "authentic doctrine has to be studied and expounded in the light of the research methods and the language of modern thought. For the substance of the ancient deposit of faith is one thing, and the way in which it is presented is another."

Come along with me, then, as I trace the adventure in understanding the Catholic faith that began for me in September of 1953, at Saints Peter and Paul School, continued over the years, and is still a big part of my life today. I sincerely hope that along the way you will gain new insights into your own faith journey, as well.

One

Everybody Has a Guardian Angel

My spouse, Kathy, and I sometimes receive invitations to speak at various workshops, congresses, or other church-related gatherings across the United States. Over the years we have noticed that the farther east we move from our home in the Pacific Northwest, the more Catholic Catholics become.

For example, we sometimes lead groups in an exercise designed to help them become more aware of the way a Catholic culture shaped everyday life years ago. We ask people to call out ways they were reminded of being Catholics when they were children. The farther east we are, the longer the list becomes.

In the Midwest and the East, people have a more pervasive Catholic culture to draw from. It's not unusual for people in these parts of the country to mention that nuns in Catholic schools instructed them to "move over in your desk so your guardian angel will have room to sit down, too."

In the Catholic schools Kathy and I attended in the Pacific Northwest, we learned that everybody has a guardian angel, but neither of us can recall being told to move over to make room for our guardian angel. Evidently, it was a widespread practice in other parts of the country. The point was to take your guardian angel seriously. One's angel was *really* there.

Even if I didn't move over to make room in my desk at school, I had no doubt about having my own guardian angel. One day in the third grade, while on my way home from school, for some reason I hopped off my bicycle in the middle of an empty lot. A high school baseball game was going on nearby, which I was aware of, but I was not watching the game. I heard a distant voice call, "Look out!" I turned my head to the right, unsure of who was calling and whether I was the one who was supposed to "look out." As I turned my head to the right, a baseball flew by so close that I felt it lightly skim the hair on the left side of my head.

"It must have been my guardian angel," I remember thinking, "who made me turn my head just enough."

Guardian angels drifted into the background as time went by. I don't remember hearing much about them in the Catholic high school I attended. In fact, after about fifth grade I gave guardian angels little thought until a few years ago.

Kathy and I were out for dinner with a married couple a few years younger than we, and the woman lobbed a question across the egg rolls and fried rice: "What should I tell our five-year-old daughter about guardian angels? Her grandmother gave her a holy card with a picture of a guardian angel, and now she's asking questions."

"Yes," her husband said, "whatever happened to guardian angels?"

Kathy and I are notorious among our friends for having committed academic theological studies. I held my disposable wooden chop sticks in front of my face and squinted at the pointed ends, as if the answer was mysteriously inscribed there in tiny letters. There were no lectures on guardian angels in graduate school.

Along with countless Catholics of my generation, and earlier, I can easily recall hearing in Catholic school about my guardian angel. One of the prayers Catholic kids were required to memorize began, "Angel of God, my guardian dear, to whom God's love commits me here . . ."

These days, guardian angels seem to have fallen on hard times. Our own children have heard little, if anything, about guardian angels in the Catholic schools they attend. *Does* each person have a guardian angel, or not?

First, let's examine a more basic question. What about angels in general? The primary source of information about angels is the Bible, and the consensus among Catholic scripture scholars is that both the Hebrew and Christian Scriptures—the Old and New Testaments—reflect a consistent belief in spiritual beings called angels.

Indeed, the Bible tells of many encounters between people and angels, and sometimes these encounters constitute a turning point in a person's life. In Genesis Chapter 16 an Egyptian slave girl, Hagar, serves Abram's wife, Sarai. Sarai is unable to become pregnant, so in accord with ancient Israelite tradition she gives Hagar to Abram "as a wife" (16:3), so that he might have children by her. Hagar becomes pregnant, and when she does she regards Sarai, who is still her mistress, "with contempt" (16:4). Big mistake.

Naturally, being the object of Hagar's contempt doesn't please Sarai one bit, so she complains to Abram, who tells Sarai that she is still in charge of Hagar, therefore she can do whatever she wants with her. Genesis tells us, with admirable restraint, that "Sarai dealt harshly" with Hagar. We may take this to mean that Sarai let Hagar know, by whatever means, who was still the boss. At any rate, Hagar takes the hint and hotfoots it out of there. A sad turn of events, but Hagar asked for it.

This is where an angel comes into the story. "The angel of the Lord found [Hagar] by a spring of water in the wilderness," Genesis (16:7) says, "the spring on the way to Shur." Most likely, Hagar was on her way to Shur to look for new employment (although we can't be Shur). The angel of the Lord says to Hagar, "Hagar, slave-girl of Sarai, where have you come from and where are you going?" (16:8)

You have to hand it to the angel of the Lord, he gets right to the point. The angel's question is one we could reflect on endlessly. Where have we come from? Where are we going? The answers you and I give to these questions reveal our true values—not what we *say* we believe is the purpose of life, but what we *really* believe is the purpose of life.

Hagar is one cool cookie. She exhibits no astonishment at being addressed by an angel, and she responds truthfully. "I am running away from my mistress, Sarai" (16:8).

Does the angel ask why? No. Does the angel argue with Hagar about the wisdom of running away? No. The angel simply says, "Return to your mistress, and submit to her" (16:9). The angel does sweeten the deal considerably. Without waiting for Hagar to raise objections, or complain that she will just get "treated harshly" again, the angel adds: "I will so greatly multiply your offspring that they cannot be counted for multitude" (16:10), which means that Hagar will have so many children and grandchildren that she won't be able to count them all.

This may sound like a dubious blessing in our era of small families. Recall that in the nineteenth century, when most Americans lived on farms, the more children you had the better, because that meant more hands to help milk the cows, feed the chickens, and bring in the harvest. This was exactly the case in the time of Abram, Sarai, and Hagar. Children were economic assets, not economic liabilities. Their approach to family life was: "The more the merrier."

The angel of the Lord continues, telling Hagar that when her child is born she should name him Ishmael, which means "God hears." The angel also lets drop that Hagar's son will grow up to be "a wild ass of a man" (16:12) who will be a difficult person to live with. He won't like anybody, and nobody will like him.

One would think that this would not come as the greatest news in the world to Hagar, but Genesis says nothing about her response, which leaves us guessing. What Genesis does say is intriguing. At this point, the text notes that it was "the Lord who spoke to her" (16:13). Genesis identifies the angel of the Lord with God himself, and right away Hagar gives the Lord a name, "El-roi," which means either "God of seeing" or "God who sees," depending on which Hebrew translator's opinion you prefer.

Either way, Hagar names the Lord "El-roi" because she is amazed. "Have I really seen God and remained alive after seeing him?" she asks (16:13). Then Hagar slogs back to Sarai and Abram, takes up her duties again, and later gives birth to Ishmael, who, if the angel's words came true, grew up to be hell on wheels.

The Hebrew Scriptures view angels as messengers of God, bringing God's word to various people. At the same time, angels often blur with God, seeming to be simply a manifestation of his presence in a particular set of circumstances.

An angel suddenly appears to stop Abraham from sacrificing Isaac (Genesis 22:11–12); an angel speaks to Jacob in a dream, but refers to himself as "the God of Bethel" (Genesis 31:11–12); the Book of Exodus (3:1–6) tells us that it was "the angel of the Lord" who appeared to Moses "in a flame of fire out of a bush" that the fire does not destroy, but later it is "God" who calls to Moses "out of the bush."

In the Hebrew Scriptures, angels sometimes serve as a stand-in for God. They are God's creatures, as we are, but they have no bodily substance. Indeed, in the telling of the story, angels often give way mysteriously to God's own presence. On the one hand, angels remind human beings of the absolute transcendence of the Divine Mystery. On the other hand, they serve to remind us of God's ongoing involvement in human affairs.

In the New Testament, angels appear in much the same ways. In Luke's Gospel, "the angel Gabriel" announces the conception of John the Baptist to Zechariah (1:11) and announces Jesus' conception to Mary (1:26). "The angel of the Lord" proclaims the birth of Jesus to the shepherds (2:9).

In Matthew's Gospel, Jesus mentions angels in connection with children, in particular. "Take care that you do not despise one of these little ones; for, I tell you, in heaven their angels continually see the face of my Father in heaven" (18:10, with some redundance there).

Angels serve Jesus after his temptation in the desert (Mt 4:11, Mk 1:13), and an angel strengthens Jesus during his agony in the Garden of Gethsemane (Lk 22:43).

A story in the Acts of the Apostles culminates when an angel frees Peter from prison (12:6–11). This "angel of the Lord" appears "suddenly," making a bright light shine in the cell. Peter is asleep, so first the angel politely taps him "on the side" to wake him up. Then the angel prods Peter along verbally, step by step, until he gets him outside.

It's amusing the way the angel must tell Peter every little move to make: "Get up quickly." "Fasten your belt and put on your sandals." "Wrap your cloak around you and follow me."

Later in Acts, Paul is shipwrecked and hasn't eaten for days, but an angel reassures him that everything will be OK. Paul says that "last night there stood by me an angel of the God to whom I belong and whom I worship, and he said, 'Do not be afraid. . . .' " (27:23).

St. Paul doesn't often mention angels in his letters, but he does say that angels witness the sufferings of Christians (1 Cor 4:9) and that angels are present but unseen at liturgical gatherings (1 Cor 11:10). Paul also insists that even angels are subordinate to the gospel: "But even if we or an angel from heaven should proclaim to you a gospel contrary to what you received, let that one be accursed!" (Gal 1:8).

One of the best known angelic events in the Gospels happens in Matthew's infancy narrative (1:18–25). Mary and Joseph are engaged to be married. Being the backward bumpkins that they are, unlike many young couples today who are "enlightened," they don't live together yet. Joseph is in for a shock, then, when Mary reveals that she is pregnant.

Joseph *knows* that he is not the father. Confused enough to want to call off the marriage, he still does not want to subject Mary to any more public embarrassment than she would already have to tolerate. So he decides to break off the engagement "privately." This is where the angel comes in.

"An angel of the Lord" appears to Joseph in a dream. Joseph, the angel says, get a grip on yourself. Don't be afraid to go ahead with the wedding. The child Mary is pregnant with, you see, is "from the Holy Spirit." The child will be a boy, and "he will save his people from their sins."

Joseph wakes up and determines to obey the angel's message. There may be some public embarrassment, but he and Mary will wed all the same. Which they do.

Later, after Jesus is born, "an angel of the Lord" (2:13) appears to Joseph in yet another dream. This time the message is that Joseph is to take "the child and his mother, and flee to Egypt, and remain there until I tell you. . . ." (2:13). The angel informs Joseph of Herod's plot to kill the infant Jesus. Again Joseph obeys the angel in his dream.

Time marches on. Matthew doesn't say how long; it could have been weeks, months, or years. After Herod's death, Joseph has a third dream. Again "an angel of the Lord" (2:19) appears with a message, only this time it happens "suddenly" (2:19). The angel instructs Joseph to take his family back to "the land of Israel" (2:20).

Joseph plans to travel back to Judea, but when he hears that Herod's son, Archelaus, took over after his father bought the farm, he has second thoughts. In a fourth dream, Joseph receives a warning, presumably from an angel again, although Matthew doesn't say this. Joseph takes a detour by way of Galilee, to a town called Nazareth.

The remarkable thing about the angel in Matthew's story of the birth and infancy of Jesus is his or her role as guardian. In each of the four instances in which an angel appears to Joseph in a dream, the angel's purpose is to protect. In the first instance, the angel safeguards Mary—especially her reputation—by assuring Joseph that it's fine for him to marry her. In the other three cases, the angel's purpose is to protect Joseph, Mary, and the infant Jesus from threats to their physical safety.

It should come as no surprise, then, that angels have a reputation in Christian tradition for being guardians and protectors. Clearly, there is plenty of biblical support for this.

Modern Catholic theology offers yet other insights. The great Catholic theologian Karl Rahner insisted in his *Theological Dictionary* that angels do exist. However, it is important to view angels only in relation to Christ. Rahner said: "We should understand the grace of the angels as the grace of Christ, Christ as the head of the angels. . . ." Angels do not complete some task left undone when the Son of God became one of us.

Father Richard McBrien, in his masterful work *Catholicism*, offers angels as an example of the spiritual realities God created. He explains that the name angels comes from the Hebrew *mal'ak* and the Greek *angelos*, which mean "messenger." The theological significance of angels, McBrien says, is twofold. First, angels help us to remember that there is more to creation than what we can see, hear, touch, taste, and smell. Second, all such spiritual beings are other than God and less than God; like us, they are created beings. Angels are not rivals of God.

History buffs, take note. The official Catholic teaching that angels exist as beings created by God comes from the Fourth Lateran Council, in 1215 A.D., and the First Vatican Council, in 1869–70.

St. Thomas Aquinas (c. 1225–1274), whose theology has had a profound impact on Catholicism down to our own time, wrote about angels in his *Summa Theologiae*. Because they are spiritual beings, Aquinas wrote, angels communicate simply "by willing to make a thought known to another."

Richard McBrien explains that angels are beings with intelligence and freedom. Therefore, they can reject God, just as we can. The Letter to the Ephesians mentions "the ruler of the power of the air, the spirit that is now at work among those who are disobedient" (2:2). The point seems to be that bad angels can influence human beings who are ready to listen to them.

The traditional story about angels goes something like this: In the beginning, God created the angels in a condition of perfect happiness, and he gave them a chance to show how grateful they were. In return, God would give the angels even greater happiness in heaven.

Some of the angels, led by an angel named Lucifer, were ungrateful wretches who refused to love God. In fact, they wanted to take God's position in heaven for themselves. As a punishment for their evil pride, God sent the bad angels to hell, a state of eternal suffering and separation from God. This is the origin, according to the story, of the good angels and the bad angels, the latter now being called fallen angels.

The purpose of this story is to explain that the spiritual world is just as much a mixture of good and evil, grace and sin, as our own world. We should keep in mind that not every "sign" or "echo" from the invisible realm necessarily comes from God.

Documented cases of persons possessed by an evil spirit, requiring the services of an exorcist, are rare. But they have occurred. Keep in mind, too, the weird activities sometimes associated with various off-the-wall religious cults, which offer an example of people who are open to the influence of "fallen angels."

One of the prayers recited by priest and people at the conclusion of the pre–Vatican II Latin Mass was a prayer to the archangel Michael: "Saint Michael, the Archangel, defend us in battle; be our defense against the wickedness and snares of the devil. May God rebuke him, we humbly pray; and do thou, O Prince of the heavenly host, by the power of God, thrust into hell Satan and the other evil spirits who prowl about the world for the ruin of souls. Amen."

Still it's important not to be "spooked" by all this. It's not as if there is a spiritual dimension just out of our reach where demons and devils are waiting for the slightest opportunity to do us harm. Recall the Christian scriptural perspective that the kingdom of God is not an entirely future reality; rather, we already benefit from its presence in our midst. Thus, any beings that might do us evil from the invisible realm are repulsed by our union with God in Christ. Ultimately, good is always more powerful than evil.

Does each person have a guardian angel, assigned to him or her by God at birth? As far as the official teaching of the church is concerned, this is a matter of personal opinion.

St. Thomas Aquinas taught that God is our primary guardian, "acting without intermediary, and instilling into [us] grace and virtue." Aquinas believed, however, that each person does have a guardian angel: "Because our present life is a sort of road home along which many dangers, internal and external, lie in wait, an angel guard is appointed for each man [and woman] as long as he [or she] is a wayfarer."

The official church calendar recognizes guardian angels by giving them a feast day of their own, on October 2. According to the *Catholic Almanac*, the feast day of the guardian angels commemorates "the angels who protect people from spiritual and physical dangers and assist them in doing good."

Historically, in the sixteenth century the Spanish held a feast in honor of the guardian angels, and in 1608 Pope Paul V extended this feast to the whole church. In 1670, Pope Clement X decreed that October 2 would be the feast of the guardian angels. Prior to all this, however, guardian angels were honored liturgically in conjunction with the feast of St. Michael the Archangel.

Today, most American Catholics trace their knowledge of guardian angels to a Catholic school. Guardian angels were taken for granted in the spiritual landscape of Catholic schools of the 1930s, '40s, and '50s. Sometimes popular piety charges ahead of prudence and common sense, of course.

Therefore, even the old *Baltimore Catechism*, with its hundreds of questions and answers, insisted on first things first. "It is a matter of faith," the answer to Question 43 declared, "that angels are deputed as the guardians of men." However, it was only *"commonly held* that each individual has a special guardian angel" [emphasis added].

Today, many Catholics seem to give little thought to having
a guardian angel. At the same time, there are plenty of mature,
well-educated, faith-filled Catholics who raise a ruckus if anyone suggests that there are no guardian angels. Indeed, according to research carried out a few years ago by the National
Opinion Research Center, in Chicago, 67 percent of the general
population believes in angels.

Jesuit Father Walter Burghardt, editor emeritus of the
widely respected Catholic journal *Theological Studies*,
suggested that the decline in devotion to guardian angels can
be traced to fewer Catholic schools and the absence of nuns in
today's Catholic schools. "They just aren't teaching kids
about guardian angels anymore, that's all," Father Burghardt
said.

Father M. Basil Pennington, a Trappist monk and author of
many books on spirituality and prayer, included the "Prayer to
Our Guardian Angel" in his *Pocket Book of Prayers*, published
in 1988. He suggested that one reason guardian angels seem to
have flown the coop is developments in recent decades in the
approach of Catholic schools to religious education. "St.
Bernard of Clairvaux [the founder of the Trappists] wrote a lot
about angels," Father Pennington said, "and I definitely
believe in them. I don't have just one guardian angel, however,
I have a whole flock of them!"

Modern short story writers, believers and nonbelievers, put
guardian angels in their stories, from Flannery O'Connor's
stories to some of the latest science fiction. Father Andrew
Greeley, sociologist and novelist, said that he definitely believes
in angels. The main character in one of his best-selling novels,
Angel Fire, is an angel who appears in the form of a beautiful
young woman. "The tradition is full of angels," Father
Greeley said, "but nobody is talking about them. I did
research on this, and even though most people believe in
angels, and angels are there in Scripture and sacred tradition,
still the theologians ignore them. I hope I have a guardian
angel. I'll be very disappointed if I find out that there are
none."

Angels are the subject of movies nowadays, too. Pupi Avati, an Italian filmmaker, in a delightful film called *The Story of Boys and Girls,* portrayed a colorful lower-middle-class Italian family. An oldest son falls in love with a young woman from a wealthy family, and the impact on their families is poignant and funny. Though he uses few explicitly religious images, Avati's film illustrates wonderfully the holiness of ordinary families.

The children in *The Story of Boys and Girls* claim to hear angels when they run down a long hill in the fields. This worries the adults, although the village priest is not so incredulous. At the end of the film, after a wild dinner that lasted hours, during which the two lovers' families met for the first time, the children escape outside to play. As they run and frolic joyfully down the hill, the camera pans along above their heads, rushing pell-mell through the trees where, Pupi Avati clearly suggests, angels fly above the children's heads.

Parents sometimes intuitively introduce their children to their guardian angel as a way to make the holy more immediate. One mother taught each of her six children to identify with a guardian angel, even to the point of encouraging each child to give his or her angel a name.

Father Edward Hays, director of Shantivanam House of Prayer in Easton, Kansas, and the author of many popular books on spirituality, recalls that some years ago he explained to a group of teenagers that angels are a literary device in Scripture to express the actions of God in the world. Then something happened that changed his mind.

"Later," Father Hays said, "I was driving along and nearly had what would have been a fatal accident. What prevented it was, a battery-powered lantern in the back of the car came on, apparently by itself, and shone into my rear-view mirror causing a really bright light, and that caused me to stop. If that hadn't happened, I would have been in a terrible accident. I went back to that group of young people and told them that I wanted to revise what I had said about guardian angels. I think some powerful force was watching over me."

At the same time, Father Hays rejects any suggestion that guardian angels look like "the religious art of my childhood tall beings in white robes with wings; that sort of thing I don't believe in."

Instead, Father Hays suggested that "we must allow the world of science to rediscover angels for us. There are entire fields of energy we haven't even begun to discover." There are more mysteries afoot in the universe than our small brains can fathom.

Some people claim to have encountered guardian angels in dire circumstances. In her collection of such stories, *Where Angels Walk*, Joan Wester Anderson tells how her son and a friend received help from what they believe was an angel.

In the dead of winter, Anderson's son and two friends decided to make what in safe driving conditions would be an eighteen-hour drive from Connecticut to Illinois, in order to be home for Christmas. The winter was harsh, driving conditions anything but safe. Weather reports cautioned against going outside even for a few minutes, it was so cold. What if Anderson's son and his friends had car trouble and became stranded someplace? She prayed, asking God to send someone to help her son.

The three young men made it to Fort Wayne, Indiana, where they stopped briefly to deliver one of their number to the home of his parents. Then the remaining two headed out again into the sub-zero weather, determined to be home for Christmas the next day. Taking a rural route to the Indiana tollway, they drove only a few miles before the car simply ceased to operate, right in the middle of nowhere. No lights were visible in any direction. The two young men began to think they were goners. The cold was so intense, they saw no way they could survive the night.

Joan Wester Anderson's son prayed, informing God that he was the only one who could help them. The two young men were sleepy, but if they went to sleep they might never wake up. Just then, two headlights appeared at the rear of the car, headlights that seemed to come from nowhere. Neither young man had seen the headlights approach.

Then someone tapped on the window at the driver's side of the car, asking if help was needed. The two weary travellers were overjoyed, and soon a man bundled up in heavy winter gear drove a tow truck around to the front of their car and hooked up tow chains. They asked the tow-truck driver to take them back to the home of their friend in Fort Wayne.

Once they arrived, Anderson's son ran inside, knowing that a hefty bill for towing awaited him. He hoped to borrow money from his friend's father. Hastening back outside to ask the tow-truck driver what the charges would be, Joan Wester Anderson's son stopped dead in his tracks. Not only was the tow-truck already gone, but the only set of tire tracks in the snow were those made by his own car.

Perhaps the reason guardian angels have fallen on hard times is a lack of imagination. "Sleight-of-hand magic," Frederick Buechner wrote in *Wishful Thinking*, "is based on the demonstrable fact that as a rule people see only what they expect to see. Angels are powerful spirits whom God sends into the world to wish us well. Since we don't expect to see them, we don't. An angel spreads his glittering wings over us, and we say things like, 'It was one of those days that made you feel glad to be alive,' or, 'I had a hunch everything was going to turn out all right,' or, 'I don't know where I ever found the courage.' "

When I learned in Catholic school, back in the 1950s, that I had a guardian angel, this was not akin to hearing about Santa Claus or the Easter Bunny. Santa Claus and the Easter Bunny are storyland characters who symbolize the benevolent secular "spirits" that dominate Christmas and Easter in our culture. Though they are benign, Santa Claus and the Easter Bunny live only in stories.

We have it on the authority of a centuries-old Judeo-Christian tradition that angels do exist, but we live in a time and a culture that find it difficult to interpret this truth in ways that make sense. If we can't weigh it, measure it, and analyze it with a computer, we find it difficult to believe it exists. For all the benefits of science, perhaps in some ways it makes us the poorer.

We may take it for granted that we're not talking about tall figures of indeterminate sex, wearing white robes, with big feathery white wings. Neither are we talking about a mere literary device in the Bible.

To adopt a minimalist approach, we're talking about benevolent spirits who, tradition tells us, act in two ways, as protectors and as messengers who sometimes convey God's word to human beings. That's the theological bottom line. From here on we must rely on our own experience and that of others.

Most people will probably never have a direct encounter with an angel in human form, although some clearly believe that this has happened to them. I recommend again Joan Wester Anderson's *Where Angels Walk.*

For most of us, there may always be some doubt about whether we have encountered angels or not. Standing on top of a high mountain, a young woman gazes at a spectacular panorama, hundreds of miles of forests and lakes spread out below her. A majestic bald eagle circles, riding the summer wind currents. The young woman felt empty during her climb. Suddenly, she feels the lightest touch on her forehead, a touch that is kind and reassuring. Her heart fills with joy. Life is good. Did the touch come from an angel? Her guardian angel?

A young boy stands on the side of a public swimming pool filled with dozens of splashing, yelling children. He tries to screw up his courage to jump in and swim across at the deepest end of the pool. He wonders if he can do it. Out of nowhere the confidence comes to him. Yes, he can do it. He jumps, he swims like mad, he makes it to the other side, triumphant. Did his guardian angel help?

No one can prove or disprove angels. But belief in angels, even guardian angels, has more going for it than against it. Consider. Would it not be wonderful if, at the wedding of a young couple, among the guests at the wedding there are, unseen, countless rejoicing angels?

Would it not be wonderful if, whenever we gather to celebrate the Eucharist, many angels join us?

Would it not be wonderful if, when husband and wife make love, their guardian angels smile and laugh, rejoicing in the divine life spouses bring to each other in their shared pleasure?

Would it not be wonderful if, while a police officer goes about his or her duties—or a farmer tills the fields, or an accountant taps the keys of a computer keyboard, or a teacher explains a math problem—a guardian angel is there, too?

Would it not be wonderful if, from the moment of conception, a baby has his or her very own guardian angel?

Would it not be wonderful if, as you read these words, an angel whispers in your ear, speaking of God's unconditional love for you, words you can hear if you listen carefully?

Maybe, to recall Frederick Buechner's words, if we expect to see angels, we will.

Two

Life Is Worth Living

Anyone who attended a Catholic school in the first half of the twentieth century—until about 1965—has etched indelibly on the tablets of his or her mind the first four questions and answers in the old *Baltimore Catechism*:

1. "Who made us?" Answer: "God made us."
2. "Who is God?" Answer: "God is the Supreme Being, infinitely perfect, who made all things and keeps them in existence."
3. "Why did God make us?" Answer: "God made us to show forth His goodness and to share with us His everlasting happiness in heaven."
4. "What must we do to gain the happiness of heaven?" Answer: "To gain the happiness of heaven we must know, love, and serve God in this world."

In the United States in this century alone, teaching nuns by the hundreds upon hundreds drilled Catholic kids by the thousands on their catechism answers. They did this because to store this information in our thick little skulls was to assure that we would understand exactly what it meant to be a good Catholic.

Let's give credit where credit is due. For many Catholic children, this simple question/answer approach to catechetics accomplished something remarkable. A Catholic kid might grow up to be a truck driver or a nurse, a farmer or a lawyer, a grocery clerk or a banker, a homemaker or a meat packer. Regardless, he or she would leave Catholic school knowing that his or her faith was reasonable. It wasn't a matter of shutting off your brain in blind faith. If the Mystery the church brought you into communion with was unfathomable, the church and its teachings and traditions were not. They combined to offer a way of life that was good.

The catechetical method Catholic schools utilized in those days relied heavily on memorization. Kids were required to memorize not only the catechism answers, but various prayers, as well. We memorized the Our Father, the Hail Mary, the Glory Be, the Memorare, the Morning Offering, the Acts of Faith, Hope, and Love, the Act of Contrition, and not a few other prayers, as well.

Once he or she left school, a Catholic young person was to know how to pray, and knowing how to pray implied having memorized certain prayers. You prayed by reciting prayers—if you memorized the prayers that enabled you to pray.

In the years just after the Second Vatican Council, particularly during the 1970s, there was a backlash among professional religious educators against the idea of having children memorize anything, prayers included. More than a few parents—products of the *Baltimore Catechism* themselves—balked at this. Today, religious education is more balanced. Text books encourage memorization of certain basic prayers, along with an approach to religious education based more on the child's personal experiences, on identifying, understanding, and celebrating God and the church in the child's life here and now.

The *Baltimore Catechism* gave us the questions and answers in one helping, whether we were asking those particular questions at that particular time or not. Boom, here they are, and now you are fully equipped to handle life, the world, and any religious questions or problems that may arise.

Today, catechetics tries to key the information to the time in the child's life when the questions arise naturally. It is based on the assumption that it makes little sense to give a child the answer to a question he or she hasn't asked yet. Today's Catholic school teachers don't tell a third grader that God is "the Supreme Being." They do not explain to young children that this means that God "is above all creatures, the self-existing and infinitely perfect Spirit" (*Baltimore Catechism,* Question 8).

Catholic schools base religious education on the conviction that no eight- or nine-year-old can possibly grasp the meaning of such words. Instead, Catholic school kids learn about God in language that makes sense to their age-level and experience.

When I think back on the years I spent memorizing the answers to the catechism questions, I know that it was not an entirely unbalanced experience. It was suitable to the era, a time when, in some ways, Catholics were outsiders in American society. We needed to be able to answer the challenges to our faith that were implicit in American society at large. We were surrounded by "heretical Protestants," and we needed to have a firm grasp on the truths of our Faith. Period.

The most basic goal of the *Baltimore Catechism,* and the most basic goal of today's catechetical programs are, when you think about it, the same. The old catechism aimed to help Catholic kids see that life has meaning and that faith and the church are basic to finding meaning in life. Post–Vatican II catechetical programs are designed to do the same.

The most basic questions any human being can ask may be stated thus: Where did I come from? Why am I here? What happens to me after I die? Catholic school catechetical programs, old and new, present kids with the Catholic responses to these basic questions. Take another look at those first four questions from the old catechism, and you'll see that this is so. Of course, there are many other topics catechetical programs discuss, but all of them build on responses to these three basic questions.

Life has meaning, and life is worth living. There is a good reason to get out of bed in the morning and go to work, even if the work you do is dreary, just a way to earn a wage. No matter how dark life may sometimes seem, there is a good reason to go on living. The entire Catholic catechetical process was and is designed to present this truth to Catholic children.

The purpose of life, I learned in Catholic schools, is to love God and other people. Therefore, life will have meaning to the extent that I accept this truth and make it the center of my existence. If I decide to live for things other than God and neighbor, I will be miserable. It's as simple as that.

I browsed through an old copy of the *Baltimore Catechism* and was surprised at how balanced it often was in the course of its 499 questions and answers. (One of the great imponderables of my childhood was: Why didn't someone think up one more question to make it an even 500?) For example, the answer to Question 190 explains how we are to love God, neighbor, and self: "To love God, our neighbor, and ourselves we must keep the commandments of God and of the church, and perform the spiritual and corporal works of mercy."

The commandments of God, that is, the Ten Commandments, are eternally relevant, although some wry wit wisecracked that today people view them as the Ten Suggestions. I suppose, on the other hand, that the commandments of the church—whatever form they may take today—have become, for better or for worse, more like suggestions than commandments.

Catholicism in the 1950s sometimes seemed like a religion of lists, and today many of the lists have little practical relevance to the life of the average person—the Seven Gifts of the Holy Ghost: wisdom, understanding, counsel, fortitude, knowledge, piety, and fear of the Lord. Others are of abiding interest mainly to theologians—the Four Marks of the church: one, holy, catholic, and apostolic.

Some of the lists we memorized still clearly relate to Christ's message about the meaning and purpose of life. The *Baltimore Catechism* declared that the ways in which one was to go about loving God, neighbor, and self were found in those two lists called the corporal and spiritual works of mercy. You don't hear much about these lists today, but they still constitute a practical guide on how to have a life worth living. Let's take a look at each list in turn.

The seven corporal works of mercy are:
1. To feed the hungry.
2. To give drink to the thirsty.
3. To clothe the naked.
4. To visit the imprisoned.
5. To shelter the homeless.
6. To visit the sick.
7. To bury the dead.

Even a cursory reading of these seven actions attests to their lasting relevance to a Christian life. Only the last is now generally out of the hands of ordinary people and in the hands of professionals, at least in our culture.

What does a person's life look like when he or she embraces a commitment to love God, neighbor, and self? Here is what it looks like, the corporal works of mercy respond. "Corporal" means "bodily," so this list is about meeting people's basic physical needs. No Christian life can ignore the need to carry out these "works," the old catechism said, and today's catechetical programs for children repeat this in their own ways.

People sometimes jump the track when they read the list of corporal works of mercy and conclude that, well, there's nothing to do but become a missionary, or work in a soup kitchen, food bank, or used clothing exchange. "I'm not a good Christian unless I spend lots of time visiting people in the county jail, or at the hospital. I must welcome homeless people into my home."

Not so fast, there, bucko. The corporal works of mercy are supposed to be lived *where we are*. Parents are prime offenders when it comes to not giving themselves credit for carrying out the corporal works of mercy regularly. What do parents do daily but feed the hungry, give drink to the thirsty, clothe the naked, care for the sick, and give shelter to those who without their parents would be homeless? Five out of seven isn't bad!

There is no reason to be entirely literal when we read the corporal works of mercy list. "To visit the imprisoned" could refer to a child who is "imprisoned" by homework and needs a parent's help. It could refer to a teenager "imprisoned" by raging adolescent hormones who needs a parent who is willing to talk about sex. There is more than one way a person can be "imprisoned." Still, what about families who live near prisons? What would happen if Christian families began to feel some obligation to reach out to those incarcerated nearby? What remarkable Catholic service organizations might develop?

Today's Catholic high schools and colleges may not require students to memorize the corporal works of mercy. But many such schools introduce students to the corporal works of mercy by requiring them to participate in a service project. I think of my own alma mater, for example, Santa Clara University, in California, where students participate in various service projects in poor neighborhoods. The same goes for the Catholic high school our children attend.

In general, the corporal works of mercy constitute a checklist anyone can use. If my life seems somehow empty or meaningless, maybe I've drifted too far from the corporal works of mercy. Maybe I need to make more time to help others.

Now let's look at the seven spiritual works of mercy. They are:

1. To admonish the sinner.
2. To instruct the ignorant.
3. To counsel the doubtful.
4. To comfort the sorrowful.
5. To bear wrongs patiently.
6. To forgive all injuries.
7. To pray for the living and the dead.

Again, we can't miss how basic this list is. Along with the corporal works of mercy, the spiritual works of mercy constitute acts of simple human caring. Anyone who does these things will have a life worth living.

As with the previous list, it can be easy to overlook the ways we already do these things in our ordinary everyday life. There is no need to earn a degree in psychology or enter a monastery to carry out the spiritual works of mercy.

Once again, parents carry out these "works" almost naturally; they are part of a parent's "job description," and not in the fine print, either. It's the wise parent who lets a child suffer or enjoy the consequences of his or her choices, which constitutes the best way to learn from experience. Along the way, any parent "admonishes" his or her child regularly.

A parent's whole life, almost, is taken up with "instructing the ignorant," which is what children are, if they are anything. At the same time, parents need to be sensitive to a child's natural tendency to have doubts, both about himself or herself, and about religious issues. Children can learn to deal with their own doubts without panic if they hear their parents express honest doubts about certain religious questions without making a federal case out of it. Doubt is no sin, after all; rather, it's one sign of a faith that struggles to grow.

If anyone knows sorrow in this world, it's children. Thus, parents regularly comfort their children, whether the cause be a skinned knee, a lost toy, or a lost friend. The death of a pet can be a deeply sorrowful experience for a child, and it's the wise parent who allows the child to grieve.

In the natural course of events, parents also must bear patiently wrongs done them by their children. It's the rare child who, at one time or another, doesn't shout at a parent amidst angry tears, "I hate you!" It's the rare child who, at one time or another, doesn't intentionally or unintentionally hurt his or her parents. When parents don't allow kids to manipulate them with such behavior, then they "bear wrongs patiently."

Some parents, when an angry child says, "I hate you," just about keel over with self-doubt and guilt. Such parents respond by trying to smooth over the situation as fast as they can. As soon as possible, they buy the kid an ice cream cone, anything to get him or her to "take back" those words: "I hate you!"

The wise parent, on the contrary, lets such words pass, knowing they mean only that the child is angry and frustrated, and perhaps with good cause. Later, when the smoke clears and the storm is over, parents set the best example when they "forgive all injuries." Helping a child learn to forgive and be forgiven is near the top of the list of the "best things ever" that parents can teach their children.

Finally, the spiritual works of mercy focus on the need to pray for one another, "the living and the dead." Today's parents read books by parenting experts. But do they pray every day for their children? Today's parents worry about their children's diets and about the impact of movies and television. We hound our children to clean their rooms and do their homework, but do we pray for them?

In her book *Coming Home*, Mennonite author Sara Wenger Shenk wrote: "A ritual that gives me courage at the end of the day, when my failures as a parent seem most vivid, is to go to the bedside of each child and pray for them one by one as they sleep. It is an acknowledgment for me that no matter how much we do as parents to care for our children, to provide for and discipline them, we are utterly dependent on the grace of God to see us through."

Of course, there are ways in which the spiritual works of mercy fit into the life of any mature Christian, not just parents. Life will have meaning, the spiritual works of mercy say, if we pray for "the living and the dead." We may take this both literally and figuratively. Thus, there may be some who are physically alive who are dead in other ways, and they need our prayers, as well.

One of the most important lessons I learned in Catholic school was that if my life was to have meaning, and therefore be worth living, I would need to distinguish between what the world might say to me and what my faith would say. I learned that for the followers of Jesus, this was no small matter. Sometimes in the Catholic schools of years ago there was too much emphasis on "the evils of the world." We would be mistaken, however, to dismiss this notion entirely.

In the Gospel of Matthew, Jesus delivers the Sermon on the Mount (Mt 5–7), which has been called "the Christian manifesto" because it reveals a tremendous contrast between the Christian way to find meaning in life and the ways promoted by "the world."

Matthew tells us that in his Sermon on the Mount Jesus addressed "his disciples" (5:1). In other words, what he is about to say here is meant for everyone who would take his words seriously as the foundation for their life.

"Blessed are the poor in spirit, for theirs is the kingdom of heaven" (5:3). Don't go to sleep! We've heard the words of the beatitudes so many times that the old brain tends to shut down at the first "blessed." Resist! Give yourself a slap in the face! Pay attention! We're talking revolution here!

If you want to have a life rich with meaning, Jesus says, then you need to cultivate complete dependence on God. That's right. This does not mean being irresponsible. It does not mean you should quit your job tomorrow and expect God to take care of all your needs. It does mean that no matter what happens, God is trustworthy, he cares about what happens to us. The challenge, for those who would have a life full of meaning, is to believe this and act on it.

We live in a culture that has gone insurance crazy, for example. Many people believe that there is no such thing as enough financial security—which implies that God is nothing but an abstraction. When Jesus says, in the first beatitude, that God will bless those who are spiritually poor, one of the things this means is that there ought to be a limit, for crying out loud, on how much and how many kinds of insurance we buy. This will vary depending on our individual circumstances, but there should come a point where we say, "No more. At this point, we stop trusting in insurance companies and start trusting in God."

What I have just said is American cultural heresy. But it also reflects a mature, responsible, adult Christian faith. If it does not, then there is no way to avoid the worship of financial forms of security.

Underlying the Sermon on the Mount, from beginning to end, is the conviction that we are called by Christ to be good Christians first, good citizens second. In fact, it is altogether possible that situations may arise where we cannot make the sign of the cross one moment, then salute our country's flag the next.

"Blessed are those who mourn, for they will inherit the earth" (5:4). Once again, Matthew's Jesus says something outrageous about how to find meaning in life. He says that God will bless those who grieve, for whatever reason.

We live in a culture that denies death at every turn, yet Jesus says that God will bless those who face up to it. The cosmetics industry turns billions of dollars a day selling the illusion of eternal youth to both women and men. Yet Jesus' words suggest that if we accept gracefully the wrinkles, the gray hair and/or loss of hair, and the weakened vision that come as we grow older—which means we accept our mortal- ity—though we mourn the passing of youth, God will bless us abundantly.

We mourn for other reasons, too. A child or spouse dies. A spouse announces that he or she no longer wants to be married. Important projects we believed in fail. We lose a job we began with high hopes. A miscarriage occurs. A child does poorly in school, despite our best efforts. For all these losses we grieve, and Jesus says that when we accept the grieving these losses naturally call for, God will bless us and life will have more meaning than before.

"Blessed are the meek, for they will inherit the earth" (5:5). You want a life filled with meaning? Jesus asks. Then try to be humble. But humility is not what we sometimes think it is.

One of the most despicable characters in all of Charles Dickens's novels is Uriah Heep, who appears in *David Cop- perfield*. Uriah Heep fawns; he grovels; he constantly engages in abject behavior. Dickens has young David describe Heep thus: "I found Uriah reading a great fat book, with such demonstrative attention, that his lank forefinger followed up every line as he read, and made clammy tracks along the page (or so I fully believed) like a snail."

"I am well aware," Uriah Heep says, "that I am the umblest person going. . . . My mother is likewise a very umble person. We live in a numble abode."

When David Copperfield remarks that perhaps Uriah will one day become a partner in his employer's law firm, Uriah responds: "Oh, no, Master Copperfield, I am much too umble for that!"

This is not the kind of humility Jesus is talking about. Uriah Heep wears a mask of servitude to manipulate people and take advantage of them. Genuine humility, on the contrary, means being honest.

Neither am I talking about a "humility" that merely masks poor self-esteem. A person who genuinely feels that he or she is incapable of doing anything worthwhile is not humble but emotionally and spiritually crippled.

Can you imgine a major league baseball superstar who is humble? A quarterback for a Super Bowl-winning football team who is humble? It's possible, but not likely. Ego seems to be a requirement these days in our sports heroes. Some, however, do exhibit genuine humility. They know they're good at what they do. But they know that basketball, or football, or baseball, are games—worthwhile, enjoyable, even worth getting "fanatical" about for the fun of it all—but hardly the most important thing in life.

John Stockton, a Catholic and a graduate of Catholic schools, was a member of the fabled "Dream Team" basketball team at the 1992 Olympics. Even on television, Stockton set a tremendous example of greatness and humility in one person. His considerable basketball skills shone, but he was quiet-spoken and more interested in what would benefit the team than what would benefit himself. Unlike certain other members of the team, he was not too good to participate in the opening and closing ceremonies, and he avoided "show-boating" to draw attention to himself.

Jesus says that God will bless those who give the credit for their gifts and talents to God and use them for the good of others. We will find meaning in life if we accept and cultivate the talents God gave us, if we don't bury them in the sand or take all the credit for ourselves.

Humililty does not mean to grovel, or to deny that we can do some things well. It means to rejoice in who and what we are, and what we can do, then find ways to be of service to others given what God gave us to work with.

When I receive a compliment, humility means saying, "Thank you, I really enjoyed doing it." It also means not allowing my head to swell as a result.

"Blessed are those who hunger and thirst for righteousness, for they will be filled" (5:6). "Righteous" is an archaic word that, in recent years, became popular among young people. As they use it, it describes something that is "cool" or outstanding; something that is "excellent," exactly the way it ought to be. In fact, this is not far from Jesus' use of the term.

Jesus says that if we would find more meaning in life, we should not just prefer that things be the way they should be, we should "hunger and thirst" for things to be that way. If we would have a meaningful existence, we should want in all situations to "do the right thing," to borrow another popular phrase.

People in our own era whose lives were based on a "hunger and thirst for righteousness" are not difficult to identify. Martin Luther King, Jr. Dorothy Day. Thomas Merton. Mother Teresa of Calcutta. Pope John XXIII. These names are well known, of course. What about those who are unknown?

Dozens of people, commonly referred to as "corporate whistle-blowers," also belong in this category. These are ordinary people who risked their jobs, and sometimes their lives, in order to report unsafe or unjust working conditions. Their primary concern was "to do the right thing," no matter what. They realized that to do otherwise would put their lives on a slippery slide toward meaninglessness.

"Blessed are the merciful, for they will receive mercy" (5:7). There is, perhaps, no more God-like act than the act of being merciful. Therefore, showing mercy to others will bring much meaning to óne's life. Yet this same act of mercy may put one at odds with many of one's fellow citizens.

Take capital punishment, for example. If recent polls are accurate, most Americans, regardless of religious persuasion— and this includes a good many Catholics, sad to say—believe that the state has the right to kill those convicted of certain crimes. The fact that every study ever done shows that capital punishment does not serve as a deterrant makes no difference.

Most people favor capital punishment because they believe in revenge, which is another word for despising a person so much we're willing to kill him or her—which is another way of saying that in some situations we believe that we have a complete grasp of the mind of God and can act in his place.

There are no grounds for such an attitude in the New Testament. To paraphrase the late Trappist monk and author Thomas Merton, all you will find in the New Testament are words about mercy within mercy within mercy. Jesus never says that we should be merciful to everyone except murderers and rapists. He never says we should show mercy to all except child molesters and serial killers. Jesus simply says that God will bless those who are merciful. Period. Can anyone imagine Jesus giving his approval to an act of legalized murder for the sole purpose of revenge, of "getting even"?

I learned in Catholic schools that there is no sin so great that God will not forgive it, and I learned that we should strive to be merciful as God is merciful. In the Sermon on the Mount, Jesus says: "For if you forgive others their trespasses, your heavenly Father will also forgive you; but if you do not forgive others, neither will your Father forgive your trespasses" (Mt 6:14–15).

"Blessed are the pure in heart, for they will see God" (5:8). Of all the ways that Jesus teaches us to live a life filled with meaning and purpose, this one, perhaps, is the most frequently misunderstood. One who is "pure in heart" is not a "goody two-shoes." That's not the point at all. Such a one is not someone who never thinks about sex; "purity of heart" carries no direct reference to sex at all. Rather, as the nineteenth-century Danish philosopher Sören Kierkegaard recognized, to be "pure in heart" means "to will one thing." To be "pure in heart" means to take as one's ultimate standard the love of God, neighbor, and self, as Jesus taught.

God will bless those who measure all aspects of their lives against this standard, Jesus said. For years, I thought this meant that in a Christian life there was room only for "serving others." To think of oneself was unacceptable because it was selfish. What I failed to see was the need to love self properly in order to love others well.

I can't give others what they need if I'm constantly stressed out. Purity of heart requires that I take time for myself, for leisure, for exercise, to "recharge my batteries." I need an annual silent retreat. I need a few minutes each day for whatever form of prayer suits me best. I can't share new ideas with others if I don't take the time to read books, magazines and newspapers. I can't write about a Christian perspective on life and the world if I don't take the time for a movie, a play, a lecture.

It takes purity of heart to see that love of God, love of neighbor, and love of self form an interdependent triad. We can't do any one well unless with do all three. But the result of keeping all three balls in the air, as it were, is a balanced life worth living.

In a nutshell, we both rely upon and cultivate purity of heart by loving God in prayer, by loving people by serving them and praying for them, and by loving ourselves, which we do by giving ourselves time to take care of ourselves.

"Blessed are the peacemakers, for they will be called children of God" (5:9). When I was a kid attending Catholic schools in the 1950s and '60s, there wasn't much talk about Catholics being peacemakers, except maybe when it came to working out playground squabbles. Still, those playground lessons come in handy because the same principles apply to national and international issues today.

I learned in Catholic schools that we needed to work out our differences on the playground without using our fists. I remember reading the story of St. Dominic Savio, the Italian teenager who stepped between fellow students on the verge of a knock-down-drag-out. He held up a crucifix between the two boys to remind them of the need to resolve their differences peacefully.

As a boy, that gesture struck me as too pietistic for an American kid. Still, I learned the lesson that being a peacemaker would give my life meaning and purpose. During the late 1960s, I wondered how many of the Catholic students active in the anti–Vietnam war peace movement had been influenced by nuns who told stories like the one about St. Dominic Savio.

Trying to be a peacemaker in the United States today is likely to put a person in a difficult position. Americans take violence so much for granted that we entertain ourselves regularly by watching dramatized violence for its own sake. Movies and television programs routinely utilize violent plots. Violent themes are often the basis for video games that appeal to children and teenagers. Not long ago, most Americans cheered wildly as military reservists from every walk of life joined full-time military personnel in a bloody war in the Persian Gulf that I believe was neither necessary nor just.

To seek meaning in life by being a peacemaker is to learn that sometimes we find meaning and purpose only at the cost of opposition from others. "Dare to be different," Sister Mildred Marie, my high school biology teacher, was fond of saying. What she didn't say was that those who "dare to be different" sometimes find themselves scorned and rejected. Like Jesus, you might say.

"Blessed are those who are persecuted for righteousness' sake, for theirs is the kingdom of heaven" (5:10). God will bless those who suffer because they are trying to do what's right. How simple this idea sounded when I was a kid in Catholic school. How complicated it became later in life.

A friend recalled that as a boy it was a matter of "daring to be different" by rejecting a neighbor boy's suggestion that the two of them steal a candy bar from the grocery store. Later, it meant something far more serious: deciding to leave a secure, high-paying job because he could no longer get up in the morning and go to work building colossal submarines designed to launch gargantuan missiles carrying nuclear warheads.

"There were people who refused to speak to me after that," he recalled. "It wasn't a big deal, because I moved to another city, but I got a taste of what it means to suffer a little for trying to do what I thought was right."

Attending Catholic schools in the 1950s and early '60s brought me face-to-face with the proposition that life is meaningless apart from faith. I learned then what my own three sons are learning today in the Catholic elementary and high schools they attend, that faith is an essential part of everyday life, not something to push off into a corner of the week. To send children to Catholic schools tells them that their faith should be a part of their everyday lives, day in and day out, week after week, year after year.

One big problem I have with sending Catholic kids to government schools—regardless of whether these schools are excellent in other respects—is the message I believe kids can't help but get from their experience there. Even without putting it into words, this choice says to our kids that their religion has only peripheral importance. From a kid's perspective, if it isn't discussed at school it must not be important, so why bother with it?

I learned from attending Catholic schools that life attains its greatest meaning when lived from the perspective of my Catholic faith, and my subsequent life experience reinforced this conviction.

I have seen the alternatives, and they are attractive, but also empty and unreliable. Some people spend their lives accumulating, or trying to accumulate, more and more money and affluence, and their lives are shallow. In our culture, millions of us embrace the consumer "religion" in place of an authentic religious faith, and shopping is their liturgy. Millions of others sincerely believe that there is no conflict between the two. But for all we buy, buy, buy, we remain dissatisfied.

In Catholic school I learned that human beings have an inner emptiness that only loving intimacy with God and other people can fill. Yet people forever try to fill it with other things: food, money, and what the French call *divertissement*, escape from the self through everything from a televison-watching habit to a drug habit; everything from socially acceptable drugs such as nicotine, caffeine, and alcohol to the use of illegal drugs.

Addressing the American Psychiatric Association, writer Kurt Vonnegut once remarked that he could imagine that psychiatrists sometimes regret having to give people a pill to wrap themselves around. Vonnegut said that he would guess that psychiatrists often wish they could give their patients a warm, loving extended family to embrace them, instead.

It was in a Catholic elementary school that I first heard some words from the *Confessions* of St. Augustine, and I believe that, in the final analysis, these words hold all the information anyone needs to have a life filled with meaning and purpose: "Our hearts are restless, O Lord, until they rest in Thee."

Three

The World Deserves Our Attention

One evening in deepest, darkest January, I received a phone call from one of our children's Catholic school teachers. "I'm calling," she said, "about your son's math work. Lately, it hasn't been going so well, and I'm wondering what we can do to stimulate better work. He's an exceptionally bright boy, and I'm sure he's capable of doing much better."

Perhaps she wasn't aware of it at that precise moment, but she echoed my conviction that only a Catholic school that educates kids well in math—as well as history, literature, writing, reading, music, and so forth—fulfills its mission as a Catholic school. This is a conviction I formed as a result of attending Catholic schools myself.

Notice I said nothing about teaching religion. It goes without saying that a Catholic school will teach religion classes, provide regular experiences of prayer, and generally cultivate an explicitly Catholic-Christian environment, one that will, ideally, supplement and support the family faith experience, which is what any Catholic school should be expected to do. Kids in a Catholic school will attend Mass together regularly. But no Catholic school can get by for long resting on its religious laurels alone.

Obviously, one big reason parents send their children to a Catholic school is to provide them with a schooling for the whole child, including his or her spirituality. But parents intuitively realize that to genuinely fulfill its Christian mission, a

Catholic school must also do an outstanding job of teaching kids all the subjects that are not explicitly religious in content. Today's more highly educated Catholic parents won't settle for anything less, and they want only teachers who are well qualified to do what they are hired to do.

The most basic reason Catholic schools must excel in teaching "readin', writin', and 'rithmetic," as well as history, literature, music, art, and all the rest, is that if they do not they are not truly *Catholic* in their approach to education. A Catholic school should touch all the bases.

The flip side of the coin is that unjust laws leave Catholic schools to scramble for the financial resources to do all this as well as it should be done. Still, most do an outstanding job with what they have to work with. Indeed, studies indicate that Catholic high schools, especially, serve their students better than government high schools do.

Catholics believe that God entered human history and became a complete human being in Jesus of Nazareth. Therefore, everything about the human situation is good and deserves to be developed to the fullest extent possible.

Since the Son of God became a human being, and participated in a human society and a human culture, human societies and human cultures carry the potential to bring us into closer union with God. Therefore, in order to be genuinely Catholic, a Catholic school must do the very best it can to prepare children to contribute to and participate in human societies and cultures.

In order to do this, a child needs to learn not only that there are seven sacraments. A child also needs to learn that $7 + 7 = 14$. It's important to memorize not only the Our Father and the Hail Mary; it's also important to memorize Lincoln's address at Gettysburg and the Preamble to the Constitution of the United States.

A kid in a Catholic school needs to memorize Robert Frost's poem "On Stopping by Woods on a Snowy Evening" and hear the story of St. Francis of Assisi. Computers have as much a place in Catholic schools as rosaries, although each have their proper time and place.

Extracurricular sports generate considerable enthusiasm in Catholic schools; but so should retreats, "searches," and projects to help people who are less fortunate. A Catholic school should help kids learn to have as much respect for the mentally and/or physically disabled as for people who are intellectually gifted or who excel as athletes. Only then can a school truly call itself *Catholic*.

The arts—including music, painting, dance, and drama—deserve not just token representation in a Catholic school, but a high priority. Otherwise, a Catholic school's claim to educate "the whole person" is an empty claim.

Over the many years I spent in Catholic elementary and secondary schools, and in a Catholic university and graduate school, I learned that all this is true. I learned that there is no area of human existence that is alien to my faith; I learned that all human endeavors have something to say to and gather from faith experience.

In Catholic schools, I learned to appreciate the music of Mozart, Beethoven, and Bach, and the films of Woody Allen. I learned to enjoy *A Midsummer Night's Dream* and *Waiting for Godot*. I learned to be on the alert for the word of God not only in the Bible but also in the classic novels of Dostoevsky and Dickens, and the contemporary fiction of Stephen King and Mary Gordon, Anne Tyler, Nancy Willard, and Annie Dillard. I look for the word of God in today's newspapers and magazines.

When I was in high school, my friend Jerry's father made his living as a painter. He worked for the local government school district, and in the summers he painted houses as an independent contractor. One hot, July afternoon I watched Jerry paint a white picket fence that surrounded somebody's house. It was a spin-off job, I suppose, that his father had gotten him. I remember thinking, as I watched Jerry paint those pickets, about something I had heard the previous spring in our religion class.

Father Kelley, our religion teacher, was an ex-marine who regaled us with stories about the "loose living" he did before he decided to become a priest. Long before it was fashionable, he had "lived in sin" with a woman, and in Hollywood, no less! As students we attributed extra authority to whatever Father Kelley said about religion, because of his past as a marine and his status as a reformed sinner.

On the day I was thinking of, as I watched Jerry slap white paint on that long picket fence, Father Kelley had said something, almost in passing, that I never forgot. He said the people who drive buses and dig ditches and build buildings contribute as much to society as do school teachers, doctors, and even priests and nuns.

I tell you, you could have knocked me over with a floppy disk, if there had been such things then. Up to that moment, I had believed that nothing anyone could do with their life could come anywhere near to being as important as what priests and nuns did. Remember this was 1961 or '62, remember, and the Second Vatican Council was barely underway. This was still the era when Catholic kids learned in school that being a priest or nun was the best thing they could be, while getting married and having a job or career was "good, but second best."

Father Kelley's words affected me like a direct revelation from God. Suddenly, I realized that he was right. Where would we be without mothers and fathers, without doctors and bus drivers, farmers and carpenters, plumbers and mechanics? Where would we be without house painters and picket-fence painters? It sounds obvious now, but thirty years ago, for me it was very big news.

"Jerry," I said, as he daubed paint into a hard-to-get-to place, "you're doing a nice job there." I remember he said, "thanks," but he also looked at me with a quizzical expression. Maybe he thought I was kidding him, when what I was doing was admiring his small but significant contribution to making our town look a little better.

In Catholic schools, I learned that the world deserves our attention because God created the world out of love and loved it enough to create it a second time through the life, death, and resurrection of his Son. I learned that we are to bring the spirit of the gospel to our work in the world, no matter what that work may be.

As the years went by, I gradually realized that not only are we to carry the spirit of the gospel into the workplace, but that our work has a spirituality. Whether our work is in an office or on a construction site, in a classroom or a space shuttle, using a stethoscope or a computer, working with others or working alone, our work has a spirituality.

The bishops of the United States said it well in their 1986 pastoral letter *Economic Justice for All*:

> The road to holiness for most of us lies in our secular vocations. . . . Our faith is not just a weekend obligation, a mystery to be celebrated around the altar on Sunday. It is a pervasive reality to be practiced every day in homes, offices, factories, schools, and businesses across our land. We cannot separate what we believe from how we act in the marketplace. . . . Holiness is achieved in the midst of the world, in family, in community, in friendships, in work.

The first time I encountered someone who consciously related his work to his spirituality was in the mid-1960s. I was a young petty officer third class in the U.S. Navy, assigned to the supply department of a Marine Corps air station at Kaneohe Bay, Hawaii. Working in the same warehouse as I was a civilian government employee whose last name was Sousa, a fairly common Portuguese name in Hawaii. I remember his name all these years later because it was the same as the famous American composer of martial music, John Phillips Sousa.

I learned one day that Sousa was a Catholic too, and during idle moments we talked about what it was like growing up Catholic in Hawaii. Sousa told me that when he graduated from a Catholic high school in 1957, he had thought seriously about entering a religious order. He had admired the brothers who taught at the school he attended, and he thought their life a good one.

Not long before Sousa graduated, he had a talk with one of the brothers he admired in particular. This brother told him that there was only one good reason to become a brother and that was for love. Any other reason wouldn't last. In a way it's like falling in love with a woman, the brother told Sousa. There's an infatuation stage, but underlying that is a more solid, long-lasting love for the religious life.

The brother went on to say that in his opinion Catholics who bring their faith *into the world* do something priests and religious can't do. Because they are "regular people," their living a life rooted in faith is more likely to have an impact on other "regular people."

Sousa said that he tried to go about his work as a supply clerk, simple as it was, with "a Christ-like spirit." Not only did he do his work conscientiously, but on the job he tried to relate to other people with kindness and respect. "Sometimes that's not so easy," he said, "especially when it comes to people I don't particularly like, or whose work habits I object to—people who strike me as lazy or irresponsible."

After a year, I was transferred to a naval air station on the other side of Oahu, but before I left Kaneohe Bay I stopped by to see Sousa. As we chatted, I thanked him for his words that day on how he brought his spirituality to his work.

Years later, I met a man—I'll call him Joe—a few years older than I who was a successful building contractor. Joe and I met in the context of a parish Bible study group for men that gathered early on Saturday mornings. Joe said that he had decided to join this Bible study group because he was feeling an emptiness in his life that he hadn't noticed before. Also, lately his marriage had been having more rough spots than usual.

The other ten or twelve men accepted Joe's remarks without question, and I think the reason was that most of them could understand from their own experience what Joe was talking about. "We're glad to have you as a part of the group," one of the other men said.

Joe's story shed some light on an issue many men and women face today. The issue is how to balance the demands of work with the need for family time and time to take care of oneself. "I had been working sixty- and seventy-hour weeks," Joe told me a few months later, after we had gotten to know each other better and his life had settled down some. "I was a walking basket case. It seemed like my wife was irritated with me all the time, and I hardly saw our teenage kids at all."

Joe said that at the same time he was making money "hand over fist." He had never earned so much money. The work was out there, and he took on more and more jobs, hiring more and more workers, and supervising everything with almost no help from anyone else.

"I realized just before I joined the Bible study group that my work was alienating me from my family. Because I was overworking, the work I was doing wasn't a good experience, either. It used to be fun, but it wasn't fun anymore, it was just a way to make a lot of money. I knew I had to do something to get my act together, something to gain control of my life again."

As Joe listened to the other men in the Bible study group talk about how they related their work and their spirituality to each other, he began to see the direction he needed to move, as well. Joe decided to set a date exactly one month in the future, and on that date he and his wife would take a three-day weekend to get away and be by themselves. He would listen to her concerns, although he already had a good idea what they were, and then he would tell her what he had in mind.

Joe's solution was to hire two assistants from among his already trusted employees. He could have afforded to do this months earlier, because his business was successful. He had been reluctant to delegate authority to anyone else. He felt that he had to keep his hands on the controls at all times. Now, he realized that this was not so. He realized that it was important for his own health, as well as the well-being of his marriage and family, to spend time with his family, as well as with his work.

"This was the best decision I ever made," Joe said. "Not only are my wife and I getting along well, but I have time to spend with my kids every day, too. And now that I have two assistant managers my business runs more smoothly than ever."

I asked Joe what all this had to do with joining the Bible study group. "As we studied the Gospels," Joe said, "I saw that relationships are at the very heart of our faith—our relationship with God, and our relationships with one another. I saw that I couldn't claim to have a good relationship with God unless I first had healthy relationships with my wife and kids."

Out of curiosity, I asked Joe if he had attended Catholic schools. He admitted that he had, right through college. "Why do you ask?"

"Just wondered," I said, smiling.

Joe cocked an eyebrow, then chuckled and said, "I see what you're getting at. Sometimes having gone to Catholic schools has an influence on us in later life in ways we don't expect."

The Second Vatican Council (1962–1965) declared that lay Catholics have a unique spirituality. "This lay spirituality," the council said, "will take its particular character from the circumstances of one's state in life (married and family life, celibacy, widowhood), from one's state of health and from one's professional and social activity" (*Decree on the Apostolate of Lay People,* art. 4).

Each of the aspects of life the Council identified, I have learned over the years, has a profound impact on a person's spirituality, whether he or she is aware of it or not. The ideal is to be aware of it.

Bill, a family physician in his mid-forties, attended Catholic elementary and secondary schools before attending a state university, followed by medical school at the same institution. I once asked Bill if I could follow him around for a day, in order to write an article for a medical magazine about a typical day in the life of a family practice physician. "Sure," Bill said, "but be ready to get up early and get home late."

The day of our appointment dawned crisp and cool in late September. I drove to Bill's home, arriving at 7 A.M., greeted Bill's wife, June, and several of their eight children as they sat around the kitchen table eating various configurations of breakfast, from cold cereal to fried eggs to frozen waffles hot from the toaster.

"Okay," Bill said, as he tightened his necktie and slipped into his sport coat. "We're off."

The first stop was a nearby hospital, where Bill had scheduled a tonsillectomy for an eight-year-old boy who had been having persistent throat infections. I donned a surgical gown and cap, slipped paper booties over my shoes, and followed Bill into the operating room, where the procedure went smoothly.

As we drove from the hospital to Bill's nearby office, I asked him if, as a Catholic, he had any reflections on his profession from an explicitly religious perspective.

"You may think it's not hard for a doctor to do that," Bill replied. " 'Healing the sick,' and all that. But the truth is that some days it's very difficult to do that."

As Bill maneuvered through the early morning traffic, he explained that the way medicine is these days a doctor has to be a sharp business person and record keeper. He said that he spends a lot of time worrying about the financial "bottom line," trying to figure out the regulations established by insurance companies, and trying to give each patient the time he or she needs, while at the same time thinking of the people cooling their heels out in the waiting room whose appointment was fifteen to thirty minutes ago.

"It's not as simple as you might think," Bill commented. He said that his spirituality of work involves struggling daily to do his patients justice "with a prayer thrown in, now and then, when the thought strikes me to pray."

For the rest of the day, I followed Bill from one examination room to another, watching as he responded to everything from a sore knee to emphysema, and from a baby's runny nose to an old woman's arthritis. At 1 P.M., we stopped for a quick lunch in Bill's office, then it was back to bouncing from one examination room to another for the rest of the day, with occasional side trips to the telephone to respond to questions from patients or to phone a prescription to a pharmacy.

At 5:30 P.M., the several persons on Bill's staff went home, while Bill sat down to check charts and fill out forms. Finally, at 6:30, Bill and I exited through the back door of his office, climbed in his car, and drove to a cafe where we munched sandwiches and drank soft drinks. Bill had a meeting to attend, and this was more convenient, this particular evening, than trying to get home for dinner.

I asked Bill to say more about his spirituality.

"It's something that underlies all that I do," he said. "It's an all-pervasive thing. Sure, it has to do with my profession as a doctor, but it's also present in my marriage and as a parent. I think it had a lot to do with the choice my wife and I made to adopt three kids from other countries, in addition to having five of our own."

In response to a question about how he balances a medical practice with family life, Bill said that he realized years ago that for him there was only one way. He sets aside two weeks every three months, and during that two weeks, he stays home. Also, he takes two two-week vacations with his family each summer. The doctor he shares his practice with fills in for Bill when he is gone, and Bill does the same for his partner when he is gone.

"My medical practice is very important to me," Bill said, "but my marriage and my family take a kind of priority. Important as my patients are, they aren't more important than my family. I realized several years ago that that means I have got to put my family on my calendar, and give them time, just as I put my patients on my calendar and give them time."

Feeling close to God, Bill said, happens sometimes when he is caring for a patient. The spirituality of his work as a physician is not so much a matter of feeling God's presence when he practices medicine as believing that God works through him when he tries to do his best.

Bill said that most of the time he feels closest to God when he is close to his wife and children. "That's where the heart of my spirituality really is."

After Bill's meeting with a Catholic school committee on sex education, he and I returned to his home at about 9 P.M. As I thanked him for sharing his day with me, and we shook hands in farewell, Bill said, "This is how my days go most of the time. But my family knows that the two-week break is coming up, and the summer vacations are coming up. And so do I."

Many people, with relative ease, can relate their work to their spirituality and even think in terms of a spirituality of work. For many others, this is not so. For countless people work is simply work, a way to earn money to put food on the table and pay the rent. Many people dislike their work, but they do it because they "have to." Many people work long hours at impersonal, even alienating jobs because they must.

"I don't like working in a fast-food restaurant, but it's the only work I can find. I don't enjoy cleaning up after people, and some of them are so thoughtless and leave such a mess."

The speaker is Norma, who is divorced and a single mother of two—a boy, age six, and a girl, age seven. Norma's job, six hours a day, is to keep a salad bar stocked and keep tables cleared and clean. It's mindless, tedious work. Norma also attends classes at a community college where she is working on an associate degree in accounting. This, she hopes, will lead to a better job in the future.

Norma dislikes her work, but she counts her blessings. She is glad to be at home in the mornings, to be with her kids and get them off to school before she leaves for work. Norma also knows she's lucky to have work at all. She knows other women in situations similar to hers who are on public assistance and can't seem to get out of the fix they're in.

I asked Norma, who is a Catholic and attended a Catholic elementary school for six years, if she sees a spiritual

dimension to her work. "As far as the work itself is concerned," she said, "the answer would have to be, 'Now and
then.' Once in a while, I can help an older person who needs
help getting stuff from the salad bar, that kind of thing."

Most of the time, Norma said, her work is just work. She
does, however, think that her motive for doing the work and
staying with the job is spiritual. "I do it for my kids, I do it
because I love my kids and I want us to have a better life some
day. Sometimes we cry about how much time I have to be away
from them, but they know it won't be forever."

Norma talked about her parish church. Distant from the
Church for a number of years, after her divorce Norma began
to pray and decided to return. She said that she and her children attend Mass every Sunday morning, and when she looks
at the large crucifix on the wall behind the altar, she thinks, "If
he did that for me, I can stick with my stupid job for my kids."

Work is many things for many people. For some, like
Norma, work relates to their spirituality not as something ful-
filling or rewarding in itself, but as a tolerable means to an
important end—namely, survival.

If there is a spirituality of work, there is also a spirituality
of unemployment. We live in a society that finds unemployment acceptable for a fluctuating percentage of the population.
Complex economic forces are at work, but the result is that
thousands of people, at any given time, are unemployed against
their will, and there is little, if anything, they can do about it.

Many Americans view the idea of guaranteed full-
employment as socialism and contrary to the free enterprise
system. The prevailing notion declares that if you are unemployed it must be your own fault; it's a moral failure, even if
your employer laid off hundreds of people, and you were one
of them.

Ted worked for the same computer manufacturer for fifteen years. One day he went to work as usual, the next day he
was unemployed, along with dozens of other people who
worked for the same company. Ted talked about what a devas-
tating experience this was: "I felt terrible—depressed, miser-

able, worthless. I felt like nobody. I was not needed. I could have been using my newfound leisure time to do constructive things around the house, but I couldn't. I just sat there feeling depressed."

Gradually, Ted "snapped out of it." Fortunately, a government program for people in precisely his predicament would pay his tuition if he returned to school. So, Ted decided to get an advanced degree in computer technology.

I asked Ted if, during the three months after he became unemployed, he saw any spiritual connections to his experience. Ted thought about it for a minute, then said, "I don't think I have ever felt so totally, absolutely dependent on God in my life. If God didn't do something for me and my family, that was it, it would be all over."

Ted said that finally it was prayer that enabled him to get out of the "blue funk" he was in. He began praying out of the depths of his feelings of discouragement and worthlessness. At first, he said, all he could do was say, several times each day as he sat immobile in a chair or stumbled around the house: "God, I'm feeling so bad. Please help me."

After a few days, Ted decided to have a talk with a priest friend who teaches theology at a nearby Catholic university. The priest listened sympathetically, then suggested that Ted try praying the rosary each morning and evening.

"I hadn't prayed the rosary in years!" Ted recalled. "I didn't even *have* a rosary! I had to go buy one."

As it turned out, the rosary was just what Ted needed. He found that its repetitive prayers had a calming influence, yet he felt that he was really praying. "Sometimes I prayed with anger, sometimes I prayed feeling sorry for myself, sometimes I prayed feeling depressed. But no matter how I felt, at least I was praying."

Ted began to look forward to praying the rosary, and soon he was taking walks while praying the rosary silently, slipping the beads through his fingers inside his coat pocket.

"I kid you not," Ted said, "the rosary was what got me back on my feet again. I started feeling hopeful, I began to feel that I was not without some power to get myself back in gear. About then, I heard about this program that would allow me to go back to school, and that was it. I was back on track."

Ted believes there is a spirituality of unemployment, and its special characteristics are more time for prayer, reaching out to ask for help from others, and learning to trust in God more completely.

"Being unemployed was what taught me how totally dependent I am on God all the time," Ted said. "It also taught me how unconditional God's love is for me. It was almost like God was glad I had lost my job, because he hadn't heard from me in so long. When you look at it that way, you could say that being unemployed was a blessing—not a feel-good blessing, but a blessing all the same."

It's rather easy to think in terms of the world's need for our concern, as Christians, as long as we confine our thoughts to the everyday, work-a-day world of jobs, careers, and even unemployment. But I learned in Catholic school that there is more to caring for and serving the world than going to work, in the usual sense. Some people are called to serve the world by working at "useless" occupations—like being artists or musicians, for example.

I was fortunate enough, as a boy, to know parish churches that were filled with beautiful stained glass windows, lots of admittedly rather maudlin statues, and liturgical music that predated the frequently impossible-to-sing music that punctuates parish Masses these days. We had some bad music back then, too, of course. But we also had more singable music than one finds in the typical parish church today.

My point is simply that I grew up in parishes and Catholic schools that exposed me to art and music, which communicated the message that being an artist or a musician was a worthwhile thing to do with one's life.

Now and then, someone comes along who carries art to illogical but sacred extremes. We might call such people "holy fools," in the tradition of St. Francis of Assisi. These are people whose main purpose in life is to play, to thumb their

noses at our awful solemnity, and say, "Hey! Let's go fly a
kite, ride a bike, fill our mouths with chewing gum and see who
can blow the biggest bubble! Let's defy convention, laugh at
the moon, sing songs out loud at inappropriate times!"

These people show concern for the world by turning it, or
at least their little corner of it, into a playground.

Such a one was Simon Rodia. Early in this century, at the
age of twelve, he immigrated to the United States from a small
town in Italy. I don't know if Rodia was a practicing Catholic,
but he came from a country steeped in Catholic culture. Rodia
had a Catholic imagination, that's for sure, because he spent
most of his life constructing a gigantic, unconventional icon
that reflected his joy at being alive.

In 1921, Simon Rodia began building one of the world's
great pieces of folk art in his backyard. Located in the Watts
section of Los Angeles, today it is known as the Watts Towers.
"I wanted to do something for the United States because there
are nice people in this country," Rodia said.

Simon Rodia had no plans, no blueprints, no master
scheme; he just started building playfully. Most of the wages
he earned working in construction, repairing telephones, and
setting tiles he spent on steel rods and bags of cement. Making
do with some nearby railroad tracks for leverage, he bent the
steel rods into various twisting and turning curves and angles.
Then he fastened these together to make spirals that wound
higher and higher into the air.

Mixing powdered cement and sand in just the right proportions, Simon Rodia made mortar. He would climb the tower
with a bucket of mortar in each hand, and when he reached the
top he would spread the mortar over his ever-higher structure.
Rodia added colorful designs by embedding bits of tile,
seashells, and stones of various hues in the mortar.

Each day, after he finished repairing telephones or setting
tiles, Simon Rodia hurried home to work on the artful towers
he loved so much. On weekends, he worked on the towers from
dawn till dusk. As he worked, he sang songs from his favorite
operas, and often he forgot about meals. On some Saturdays

and Sundays, he rode the streetcar to the beach to collect seashells. When Rodia couldn't afford to pay to ride the streetcar, he walked several miles to the beach, then carried his heavy collection of shells home in a sack.

Rodia used broken dishes to make flower shapes in the mortar of his towers. Green glass from broken 7-Up bottles decorated his birdbath. Rodia's growing tower fascinated him. After a while it became its own scaffold, so he could climb the towers themselves to work on the towers.

Simon Rodia said that he was inspired to build his towers by great men he read about in a set of encyclopedias he owned. He talked about Michelangelo, Columbus, Galileo, Marco Polo—and one American, Buffalo Bill Cody.

Thirty-three years after he began, in 1954, Simon Rodia stood back and admired three tall towers—the tallest of which was almost 100 feet high—and four smaller towers. He often called the three tallest towers the Nina, the Pinta, and the Santa Maria, after the three ships Columbus sailed in. Under the towers, Rodia built a model ship which he called "the Ship of Marco Polo."

Rodia added three fountains, a birdbath, decorated pathways, and a fancy gazebo, to make a cement, mortar, glass, and seashell "garden of structures" under his towers. Then he built a scalloped mosaic wall to separate the garden and towers from the street. Simon Rodia decorated every square inch of his playful creation with stones, shells, and bits of glass. But he also used old faucet handles, cookie cutters, and tools. Rodia had no thought for what others might think would look good; he simply "did his own thing" and rejoiced in it.

In the early years, neighborhood children shared Simon Rodia's dream. They helped him to gather broken glass and stones, and Rodia paid the children a penny apiece when they brought him old plates he judged to be beautiful. As time went by, however, and Rodia's project grew, his neighbors decided he was nothing but an eccentric old man with strange ideas.

As they will do, the children took their cues from their parents and began to taunt Simon Rodia. They vandalized his work. Still, Rodia continued to labor on his towers because, he said, he wanted to finish what he had started. Rodia looked at his towers and at the cement and mortar "garden of structures" below them. He watched the countless bits of glass and seashells sparkle in the sun, and he believed that what he had done was beautiful.

Finally, a day came in 1954 when Simon Rodia grew weary of the conflict with his neighbors. So, in true Franciscan fashion, he simply gave his house and his towers to a neighbor, packed his few possessions, and moved to northern California to be with relatives.

After Rodia left, people argued over his towers. Some said they were unsafe and should be torn down. The building inspector of the city of Los Angeles called them "the biggest pile of junk I've ever seen, a king-sized doodle, an eyesore that should be pulled down!"

For another five years, Simon Rodia's towers and garden were vandalized, and his little house was burned down. Then in 1959, two men bought the towers and planned to restore them to their former glory. But when they applied for a building permit, they discovered that the city planned to demolish the towers because they were judged to be a safety hazard. This was incredible, because in 1933 the towers had remained standing and solid when an earthquake leveled everything around them and even made the city hall tremble, which was ten miles away!

Other people appreciated Simon Rodia's vision, so they formed a committee to prove that his towers were solid and a threat to no one's safety. On October 10, 1965, a machine designed for such purposes put 10,000 pounds of pressure on Simon Rodia's towers. This pressure was equal to a seventy-mile-an-hour wind. The result: one tiny piece of mosaic tile fell off. The towers were so strong that the machine applying the pressure began to bend, so the test was stopped. This was enough to convince the city of Los Angeles that Simon Rodia's towers were safe.

"You have to be good good or bad bad to be remembered," Simon Rodia once said. Today countless tourists and school children visit the Watts Towers every year. Simon Rodia expressed his love, care, and concern for the world in an unconventional way, but a way that was "good good," all the same.

In Catholic school I learned to appreciate people like Simon Rodia and all the ways people contribute to the good of the world through their everyday occupations.

Four

We're All in This Together

"We're sending our kids to that particular Catholic high school because we know that they will get an outstanding education there; they'll be well prepared for college, which will put them on the road to success in a career later on."

As I listened to the man who spoke these words, I realized that our oldest son would attend the same high school for a different reason. Sure, we wouldn't send our son to this Catholic high school unless it would give him an excellent secondary education, academically speaking. But our most basic reason was different.

I once asked myself what it was about the Catholic high school I attended in the early 1960s that had the biggest impact on my life. I realized that although I gained worthwhile knowledge in subjects such as English, math, biology, religion, and history, it wasn't the classes that had the deepest impact on my life. It was the Catholic cultural environment that affected me the most. More than that, it was the Catholic community in the high school I attended that stayed with me. We didn't use such terminology then, but it was the experience of a Catholic high school faith community that touched my heart.

The high school I attended, DeSales High School, in Walla Walla, Washington, was no great shakes academically in the early 1960s. In fact, it was second-rate. My friend Jerry had to enroll in an evening class at the local government high school in order to take mechanical drawing. The extracurricular activities were meager, too. I was on the yearbook staff, and I helped out with the student newspaper. There was no music program to speak of, and no drama classes. Guys like myself, who were not interested in playing football or basketball, or who didn't get excited about track, were out of luck in the sports department. There were no baseball or tennis teams.

I earned a letter in sports by becoming what was known euphemistically as the manager of the track team. This meant that I distributed uniforms and towels, washed same, and cleaned up the locker room after practices. I also went along to track meets at other schools to carry equipment. As we said in those days, "big fat hairy deal."

For all its weaknesses, however, DeSales High School served an important purpose for me: it met my need to belong and to find meaning in life. In today's lingo, I needed a "sense of community," and I found it in a Catholic high school. The spiritual life of the school touched me in a way that lasted.

This is the main reason we chose a Catholic high school for our oldest son, and this is the main reason his younger brothers will attend the same high school. Without a deeply rooted religious faith as a foundation, one's life can go terribly awry, no matter what other knowledge and skills one may accumulate along the way. We want to give our kids every opportunity to embrace such a faith. Not that a teenager is guaranteed to be a faith-filled Catholic just because he or she attended a Catholic high school; that role goes to the family. Still, families need all the help they can get, and a good Catholic high school can be a big help.

We want our kids to learn their academic lessons in a Catholic social context. We want them not only to address the religious issues appropriate to their stage of development in religion classes. We want them to attend retreats and searches with their peers. We want them to have the opportunity to attend Mass during the week with their friends. We want their faith tradition to be integrated into their daily experience of school, not privatized—and thus rendered more or less irrelevant—by being restricted to home and parish.

During my four years in a pre–Vatican II Catholic high school, I learned the post–Vatican II lesson that together we *are* the church. I learned that we're all in this together, and I learned that there is no better reason to hope. We want our three sons to have the same experience, only more so.

Peter L. Berger, a Lutheran sociologist, wrote a book that I read in college called *The Sacred Canopy.* Berger said that from a sociological perspective we may tag Christian believers—those who genuinely try to base their lives on their faith, not the "Sunday Christian" or "baptized unbeliever" varieties—as "cognitive deviants." This simply means that one who takes his or her Christian faith seriously thinks in a way that deviates from the perspectives of the dominant culture, which is indifferent to religion, at best, or, at worst, embodies values and attitudes that conflict with a Catholic-Christian world view.

Those who take their faith seriously are cognitive deviants, they think in ways that lead them to act contrary to the dominant culture. It is not easy for someone to continue in their cognitive deviancy alone, Berger said. We need other cognitive deviants to support our cognitive deviancy, otherwise we are likely to begin thinking and living like unbelievers. This is one of the main reasons for parishes and other faith communities. We're all in this faith thing together, and we need to support one another.

This insight becomes even more important when we realize that today we live in a culture that moved in recent decades from religious neutrality to religious indifference or, in some instances, outright antagonism to religion. Until the late 1960s, the dominant culture expected you to practice the religion of your choice, but you were also expected to keep it to yourself. Today the dominant culture doesn't care if you have a religion or not, but if you do you had better keep it to yourself because it has nothing to do with anything in "the real world." If a person does bring his or her religious convictions into the public forum (e.g., on the abortion, capital punishment, or euthanasia issues), he or she is likely to encounter angry opposition. "Stop trying to force your religion/morality down my throat."

In such a social context, Catholic high schools offer a distinct alternative, a learning environment that is not only open to but actively encourages a Catholic-Christian cognitive deviancy. A Catholic school takes for granted that no outlook on life makes sense apart from a foundational commitment to love of God and neighbor, and apart from participation in the liturgical, social, and intellectual life of the church.

Given the present cultural antagonism toward bringing a religious perspective into the public forum, Catholic schools encourage young people to see that everyday life, "the real world," is *precisely* where faith belongs, otherwise faith becomes little more than a spiritual aspirin.

Membership in a Catholic high school community of faith led me to consider basic questions about the meaning of life. This may be possible in a government high school, but with no common faith heritage to suggest some clear responses to the questions, a kid has only his or her own resources, which can lead to a moral relativism that leaves a kid more confused than ever.

One of the resident "characters" on the faculty of DeSales High School was Sister Mary Aquinas. Seventy if she was a day, tall and lean, with pale blue eyes that twinkled with intelligence behind rimless glasses, Sister Mary Aquinas thought it important to get her sixteen-year-old sophomore English students to face their mortality. To this end, she required us to memorize Emily Dickinson's poem which begins, "Because I could not stop for death, / he kindly stopped for me. . . . "

Long before I read Elisabeth Kubler-Ross' widely influential book, *On Death and Dying*, in college, I had thought about my own death and reflected on its meaning. Given that I am going to die, what should that teach me about how I should live? Today's dominant culture might view the idea of encouraging sixteen-year-olds to think about death as morbid and unnecessary. On the contrary, conducted in the context of a Catholic high school faith community it was a liberating experience.

Reflecting on this question in the light of my Catholic faith tradition, both in Sister Mary Aquinas's class and since, I arrived at conclusions that gave my life more meaning, not less. I became more hopeful, not morbid. I learned that to reflect on one's mortality is to put one's life in its proper perspective. It becomes easier to relax, to avoid stress, and to enjoy being alive.

A newspaper article told the story of a mother who had to tell her eight-year-old daughter that she had a form of brain cancer that could not be treated. She would die in a matter of weeks. The little girl listened solemnly, then turned to her younger sister, smiled and said, "Let's go play!"

What more appropriate response to the news of one's imminent demise? Or of one's mortality? From the Catholic high school faith community I belonged to I learned that since I am not going to live forever, there is little worth knocking oneself out for apart from the love of God and neighbor and a general dedication to rejoicing in the gift of life. I learned that the ideal is to face pain and sorrow, life's dark times, with courage and with a minimum of whining, in order to go on living for those things that are worth living for: above all, God and other people.

Participation in Catholic school communities of faith prepared me for the future of the church in more ways than one. I learned on an experiential level that the church is, first of all, people.

As a child, I memorized the *Baltimore Catechism*'s answer to the question, "What is the Church?" Thus: "The Church is the congregation of all baptized persons united in the same true faith, the same sacrifice [i.e., the Mass], and the same sacraments, under the authority of the Sovereign Pontiff and the bishops in communion with him."

The old catechism definition is not as paleolithic as some might think; it does, after all, start off by saying that all baptized Catholics, not just the hierarchy, constitute the church. All the same, some ten years after this definition was etched indelibly on the tablets of my mind, the Second Vatican Council adopted a thoroughly people-centered and more inclusive point of view.

In 1964 and 1965, the council issued its two major documents on the church, the *Dogmatic Constitution on the Church* and the *Pastoral Constitution on the Church in the Modern World*. Both of these documents discussed the church in Scriptural terms, as first of all "the people of God" (for example, see the *Dogmatic Constitution*, art. 9; see also 1 Pt 2:9–10). To say that the church is, at its most basic, all of us together is to say that all of us are responsible for *being* the church.

The Second Vatican Council also downplayed the "one true church" language that characterized Catholicism for about 500 years prior, since the Council of Trent. Trent was dominated by the perception that the church had to defend itself against the inroads of the Protestant Reformation. In a different mood entirely, the Second Vatican Council said a good deal about the need for ecumenical efforts, and it dubbed Protestants our "separated brethren" (see, for example, the *Decree on Ecumenism*, art. 8).

Another insight in the two documents on the church years later had a profound impact on my life. That insight appeared in these two documents as an observation that the family is the "domestic church," which simply means "home church."

My wife, Kathy, and I were hired in 1978 to direct the family ministry efforts of our diocese. We were responsible for marriage preparation programs, ministry to separated and divorced Catholics, parenting education, marriage and family enrichment, and programs on family spirituality. As time went by, I began to wonder about the significance of what we were doing.

Having served earlier as full-time directors of religious education in parishes, we were convinced that one-hour-a-week religious education programs (CCD) were largely a waste of resources. But how, exactly, did family ministry offer a more worthwhile alternative? We were in the process of beginning our own family at the same time, so I sensed in my bones that what we were *about* was important, but I wanted to understand *why*.

Reading articles and papers written by others involved in family ministry around the United States, and discussing shared concerns with other family ministers at national meetings, I began to realize the tremendous significance of calling a family a "domestic church."

I began to understand that the most basic form of faith community most people experience is some form of family life. I learned that this is an aspect of the theology of the church that the vast majority of pastors, bishops, and theologians overlook. I also learned that to dismiss the family as the foundational church is to put at risk the future of our parishes and, so, the future of the church as a whole. But I'm getting ahead of myself. . . .

As a student in a Catholic high school, where Catholic faith and culture were woven into the fabric of my everyday social and academic life, I learned from experience that relationships are central to a person's identity. Blessed with friends and teachers who cared about me, I learned that relationships can make a tremendous difference in a person's life. Years later, this insight came together with what I experienced in family ministry and in my own family life, and I realized that the church needs to nurture family life and friendship.

Through my activities in family ministry, I learned some fascinating facts. I began to recognize that the Hebrew Scriptures are filled with stories about families and family relationships, many of them stories about families that rival the wonderful or terrible stories we hear about families today. Recall the stories in the Book of Genesis alone: Adam and Eve,

Cain and Abel, Abram and Sarai, Abraham and Isaac, Isaac and Rebekah, Jacob and Esau, Moses and the Flood—family stories, all. Why would the Bible have so many stories about families and family relationships, I wondered, if family life isn't foundational to our relationship with God?

I talked with a rabbi who assured me that in the Jewish tradition the home, not the synagogue, is where the most important religious events take place. Sabbath, Passover, you name it—it happens as a family observance first. Our Christian roots are in Judaism, I knew, so where along the way did the parish become the bottom line, instead of the home?

I learned that one of the strands of thought that runs consistently through the entire New Testament says that our relationship with God cannot be separated from our relationships with one another. Love of God and neighbor are inseparable, so we need to do both. Not only that, but to love one is to love the other. Therefore, family relationships must be at the heart of our relationship with God.

Jesus says that where even two or three gather together in his name, he is among them. To recognize this is basic to any complete theology of the church. What is a Catholic-Christian family if not two or three gathered together in his name?

I discovered how basic home settings were in the early church. The early Christians gathered in one another's homes to pray and celebrate the Eucharist. Catholic scripture scholars I read who are married and parents themselves declared that in the early church the family was the most basic form of faith community.

One of the earliest Christian theologians, St. John Chrysostom, wrote in the late fourth century that the family is *ekklesia*. This is the Greek New Testament theological term for "Church." Chrysostom didn't say that the family is "like the church," he said that the family *is* the church in its smallest form.

I learned that Christians took for granted for centuries that the first place they were to live their faith was in their everyday life, in their families and in their work. During the Counter-

Reformation period, in the sixteenth century, the church made a major "turn to the parish." In order to defend the church against the onslaught of the Protestants, church leaders believed that they had to bring every aspect of Catholic life under institutional control.

If important, even basic religious experiences during earlier times happened in the home, now the center of Catholic faith and practice was the parish. If before the Reformation and Counter-Reformation parents were the main religious educators of their children, now the parish priest had that distinction.

I came across a quotation from Pope Leo XIII, the first of the modern popes. In the late nineteenth century, he called the family "the first form of the church on earth." It wasn't until the Second Vatican Council, in the mid-1960s, that the idea surfaced again. As I mentioned above, the Council dubbed the family "the domestic church," the church of the home.

In a nutshell, I learned that our family relationships, whatever form they may take at a particular point in our life, are central to the life of the parish, and so to the church as a whole. In the course of a visit to the United States, Pope John Paul II said that family life is "the very substance of parish life." Parishes should have a major orientation towards the pastoral support of family relationships of all kinds, the pope said.

At the same time, I concluded, because families are meant to "constitute the Church in its fundamental dimension" (John Paul II), families have a responsibility to support their parish. Families and parishes have an interdependent relationship. They need each other. The way things are for families in our society today, however, the ball is in the parish's court.

Families experience a tremendous degree of stress and pressure from many sides today. They need the support and encouragement only their parish can offer. If Catholic families don't get the support they need from their parish they will look elsewhere. It's as simple as that.

In 1989, an ad hoc committee on marriage and family life, organized by the bishops of the United States, issued a document called *A Family Perspective in Church and Society*. This document calls for parishes to adopt a family perspective on all aspects of parish life, from liturgy to religious education, from finances to visiting the sick.

The reason we need a family perspective is that the place we experience our relationships with God and neighbor most commonly is in our homes with other family members. From a faith perspective, "we're all in this together" applies first of all to family life. Our most basic experience of a faith community happens not in our parish church but in our homes. From this fact we must conclude that when the quality of our faith experience is good at home it will be good in church.

This is true for single people, as well. Single adults continue to belong to an extended family network, and these relationships have a major impact on their lives. Relations with aged parents who need extra care and attention, relationships with married siblings who may think of their single brother or sister as a built-in babysitter, all such family relationships affect single people's lives, and they need help from their parish to cope with them in a creative and loving manner.

If we view families of various kinds—single-parent families, traditional two-parent families, blended families, single people in the context of their extended family relationships—as the church's foundational units, then as family life goes, so goes the church. Perhaps no group is more aware of this than Catholic school teachers.

Talk with any teacher in a Catholic school and he or she will tell you that a Catholic school can do best what it is supposed to do when a child's family does what it is supposed to do. The most obvious example is religion. Religion classes will have an impact if the child comes from a family that lives its faith every day, in the normal course of events. If a child comes from a family that limits its religious expression to an hour on Sunday morning, religious instruction may slide off the child's psyche like the proverbial water off a duck's back.

The same is true of the schooling experience in general. A child will do well in school if parents support the teacher's efforts. A child will do his or her best when that child experiences a home life that is as healthy as possible. Therefore, from the perspective of Catholic schools, as well as parishes, it makes sense for the church to care about family life enough to give it more than the occasional official document; parishes need to actively nurture family life, celebrate it, and proclaim its value and importance at every opportunity.

In Catholic elementary and secondary schools, I experienced the value of a living faith community, and later I applied what I had learned to family life. The same insight applies to other forms of faith community that have been important to me over the years, including the parish.

During the 1950s and early 1960s, I grew up in parishes that were typical of the church in the Pacific Northwest. In our part of the country, we never had priests and nuns in the huge numbers that the East and Midwest took for granted. As a result, what today we call "lay ministry" has never been unusual for us.

In Oregon, Washington, Idaho, and Montana, we have never experienced the tight parish-neighborhood identification that has existed for so long in cities such as Chicago, Philadelphia, and New York. If asked where he or she was from, no Catholic kid in Portland, Seattle, Missoula, or Boise would give the name of a parish.

Consequently, if anything, the post–Vatican II problem of adopting a consumer mentality with regard to one's parish has been even greater for us than in parts of the country with a more pervasive Catholic culture. Not that the Catholic consumer mentality is absent in other parts of the country. I believe that this odd approach to parish life is common in all parts of the United States today.

Many Catholics of good will bring an attitude to their parish that is similar to the attitude they bring to a shopping mall. One goes to the mall to meet needs or desires for clothing, entertainment, groceries, and lawn care products. One goes to one's parish to meet needs of a spiritual nature. This is a consumer mentality, one which says, "I have a need or want, so I will go to the mall and get what I need to fill that need or want. The supplier and I have no significant relationship."

The trouble with this mentality when we bring it to our parish is that a parish is not supposed to function like a spiritual K-Mart. Priests and other parish ministers are not there to dispense spiritual fuel, in the form of the Eucharist and other sacraments, and various religious programs and services, much as a convenience store gas station dispenses gasoline for your car and potato chips for you.

In Catholic schools I learned that the church is a community of people who share a common faith and gather for mutual support and encouragement in various liturgical, social, service-oriented, and educational contexts. Today, too, a parish is supposed to be a community we participate in, a community we belong to not only because we have a need to receive, but also because we have a need to give. The trouble with bringing a consumer mentality to a parish is that it short-circuits the life of the parish community.

The more people who show up for Mass on Sunday mornings or Saturday evenings with a consumer mentality, the less likely that parish will be the community of faith it is supposed to be. At the same time, I believe that there comes a point where many of today's parishes, made up of hundreds of families and other households, can no longer be the faith community they are supposed to be unless parish ministers work to overcome the impersonality that comes so easily with huge numbers of people.

As important as parishes have been to me over the years, I always felt that I had experienced something in Catholic school, from elementary school through graduate school, that I could never find in a parish. As time passed, I gradually realized that I was missing the experience of a small faith community.

Early in the life of our own family, Kathy and I were fortunate to find ourselves involved with a loosely structured small faith community that we still cherish many years later. This small faith community of some dozen families is organized around a common dedication to serving engaged couples.

Our diocese began sponsoring a weekend-format marriage preparation program in the early 1970s. Married couples were recruited to serve as team couples. As time went by, these couples began to gravitate toward one another to give and receive support for their marriages and in their role as parents of growing children. We all participate in the life of our respective parishes, but we find that our small community meets needs that our parishes do not.

Over the years, our community served various purposes. When our children were babies and young children, we organized a babysitting co-op, trading points instead of money. If you took care of our kids for two hours this week, we would care for your kids for two hours next week.

From time to time, we organize evenings to get together and listen to a presentation by one expert or another on topics related to marriage, parenting, and family life.

Once or twice a year, we assemble for a home Mass, to mark some special occasion. Most of the time, our shared prayer means gathering one evening a month, each time in a different family's home, for prayer and social interaction. The centerpiece of our prayer is a modified form of the rosary, but our prayer time also includes music, silence, lighted candles, perhaps some readings from the Bible or a book or article, and time to mention various prayer intentions. We are particularly sensitive to various marriage and family issues during our prayer.

Over the years, we have prayed for friends or relatives of couples in our group who are having a difficult time with their marriage, who are going through a separation or divorce, who have serious illnesses, or have died. Of course, we also pray for ourselves and our families.

All of these activities, the prayer times, the social get-togethers, the mutual support, are good. But we realized long ago that none of these things is what holds our small faith com-

munity together. As I mentioned above, what brought us together in the first place was involvement in a program designed
to help engaged couples prepare for marriage. This common
commitment to a form of service is the glue which holds us
together.

Now and then, someone asks me how they can get a small
faith community organized, and I always respond that the first
thing is to find a need that those who join can buy into. It may
be a marriage preparation program, or it may be helping out at
a soup kitchen or a shelter for the homeless. It may be cleaning
a parish church, or it may be supporting a home for develop-
mentally disabled children. The opportunities are endless, but I
believe that a small faith community must have service as its
foundation if it is to last.

People sometimes decide to organize a small faith community around prayer. "We'll get together to pray." I have
never seen such an effort succeed. Neither do small faith communities based only on a desire for social interaction seem to
last. I have seen the same with those who would make some
form of adult religious education the basis for their small faith
community.

All of these goals are good, and they can all be a part of a
small faith community's experience. But a shared dedication to
reaching out to serve others who have some special need seems
to be the only thing that will provide a lasting foundation for a
small faith community.

Parishes sometimes attempt to establish small neighborhood groups in order to give parishioners opportunities to
share and grow in their faith with a small community of other
people. Renew, a widely used parish renewal program, utilizes
small groups. By and large, these parish-organized small
groups seem to attract a limited number of people, and they
fizzle out as time goes by.

I suspect that such small faith-sharing groups overlook the
need for a family perspective, and they aren't service-based
They presume that the small faith-sharing group is the parish's
bottom line, when in fact people's family relationships are

where they daily experience the cross and resurrection of Christ. These small groups depend on a "faith-sharing" process that involves some prayer and much talk, but little active love of God and neighbor. If a small faith community addresses people's family-related issues, and if it is service-oriented, then it will thrive.

That's the small picture, if you will. There is also the big picture. In other words, thinking of myself as a member of a parish and of a small faith community depends on thinking of myself as a Catholic in a much larger sense.

Attending Catholic schools has had a great deal to do with the fact that I am a practicing Catholic today. I am a Catholic, a member of the worldwide Roman Catholic Church. What this means to me has changed over the years. When I was a child in elementary school, I knew that the pope had a special place of leadership in the church, and I knew that the church's "main office," as it were, was the Vatican, in Rome. I remember that Sister Angelica, the Benedictine nun who was my teacher in the third and fourth grades, made much of the idea that the Catholic Church was "the one true Church."

Later, as a student in a Catholic high school, I took pride in the fact that I was a Catholic, but my understanding of the church was still rudimentary and unsophisticated. "The church" was, first of all, the church's leaders, the pope, the cardinals and the bishops. If "the church" taught something, that had nothing to do with me, except that I was to listen and obey.

Later, as a Religious Studies major at a Catholic university, and as a graduate student in Theology at yet another Catholic university, my grasp of "the church" deepened and became much broader. I began to see the implications of the Second Vatican Council's declaration that the church is, first of all, the People of God.

Today, being a Catholic means to me that I belong to one church that finds a variety of expressions all over the world, in various societies and cultures. I know from personal experience that the Catholicism I find in Boston or Philadelphia feels different from the Catholicism I find in Spokane, Washington, or Eugene, Oregon. The church in Los Angeles feels different from the church in New Orleans. Naturally, then, the church in Africa will fit African cultures, and the church in Japan will find expression in ways that make sense to the Japanese. Still, in all these places what I will find is the Catholic Church.

One of the finest aspects of being a Catholic today, I believe, is how sympathetic both ordinary Catholics and church leaders are to ecumenical concerns. I believe that one day there will be some form of unity-in-diversity among the mainline Christian churches. In the mean time, it is always gratifying to hear a Lutheran minister or Episcopal priest speak from the pulpit in a Catholic Church, or to hear a Catholic priest preach from the pulpit in a Protestant church.

Catholics believe that the pope and the bishops exercise a special form of authority to teach and guide the church. At the same time, the church is a human institution and, as such, it flounders. Church leaders sometimes make mistakes, and I reserve the right to object and argue and criticize. But I do so as one of the family. Just let someone who does not love the church start criticizing, and watch how fast I rush to the church's defense. Even if I agree with a particular criticism, I'll point out what a minor issue it is compared to the many benefits and blessings that come with being a Catholic.

Attending Catholic school, I learned what spiritual nourishment comes from participation in the liturgical, social, and intellectual life of the Catholic Church. I learned to appreciate the ways that this happens on the local level, in my own parish and small faith community. But I also learned that local church communities draw their life from a tradition that resides in a worldwide institution that is older than any other in the Western world.

Being a member of the Catholic Church is, today, something I am proud of and grateful for. It's a wonderful feeling to know that we're all in this together.

Five

Life Needs Prayer
Like a Tree Needs Water

The morning of November 22, 1963, was like any other in my senior English Literature class. I don't remember what we were discussing, but suddenly Sister Anna Clare, the older nun who taught the girls "home ec," burst through the door and whispered something to our young teacher, Sister Mary Christina. She said, rather off-handedly, that there was a rumor that President Kennedy had been hurt, but she didn't give the rumor much credence.

We students looked at one another in confusion. Because I sat near the back of the room, I didn't hear clearly what had been said. Sister Mary Christina tried to go back to whatever she had been talking about, but soon over the intercom speaker in the back of the room came the voice of the principal, Father Edward Caffrey. Father Caffrey announced that according to news reports, President Kennedy had been shot while visiting Dallas, Texas. He then switched the radio on over the intercom system, and we listened in horror as a news announcer gave a description of what was happening in Dallas. The president had been shot, but no one knew if he was alive or dead.

We continued to listen as the announcer repeated, over and over, all that he knew, and added bits of information as he received them. The moment he announced that President Kennedy had indeed been killed, I happened to glance in the direction of one of the girls in the class. She was an attractive girl named Mary, with dark hair and eyes and a pleasing personality. At the announcement of the president's death, she jumped in her seat, gasped, and began to cry.

This was, without question, the most earthshaking event I had ever experienced. My perceptions of life and the world would never be the same again. Nothing was as safe and reliable as I had thought. Later, I wondered how government school administrators had handled this situation. In a Catholic high school the response was obvious. In a matter of minutes, the entire student body assembled in the school gymnasium for Mass. Clearly, what one did at a time like this was gather with others to pray.

Prior to this, during my sophomore year, a recent graduate of our high school was in a terrible automobile accident. The faculty organized an around-the-clock weekend prayer vigil for him, and we students signed up to be in the school chapel for one hour during this weekend. We prayed for the former student's recovery, and I was very impressed, indeed, when word came the following Monday that he had come through surgery successfully and would have a complete recovery.

From my first days in Catholic school, prayer was a taken-for-granted part of each and every school day. We not only prayed, but we were expected to understand prayer. One of the definitions from the *Baltimore Catechism* that Catholics who grew up in the '40s and '50s never forget is the response to Question 475: "What is prayer?" Answer: "Prayer is the lifting up of our minds and hearts to God."

As we shall see, there is much more to be said about prayer, but in its favor we must admit that the old catechism definition took for granted that prayer means relating to a transcendent God, and that prayer is a communal action. In prayer we lift up "*our* minds and hearts to God." Even when we pray alone, the catechism implied, we pray in union with the entire faith community of the church. This is in contrast to the popular belief that prior to the Second Vatican Council Catholic spirituality was totally individualistic. Privatized much Catholic piety certainly was, but behind the definition of prayer every Catholic school kid memorized there was a communal assumption.

At the same time, in "the old days" we tended to identify prayer with the recitation of preformulated prayers. Catholic school kids memorized prayers up the kazoo! Here is but a partial list of the prayers we knew by heart: The Sign of the Cross, the Lord's Prayer, the Hail Mary, the Glory Be to the Father, the Apostles' Creed, the Confiteor, an Act of Faith, an Act of Hope, an Act of Love, the Act of Contrition, the Morning Offering, the Angelus, the Hail, Holy Queen, the Blessing before Meals, and Grace after Meals.

This approach to prayer clearly implied that one prayed by saying previously memorized prayers. Today's Catholic school kids memorize prayers, too, but not so many. They learn that to "say prayers" does not automatically qualify as praying. It's perfectly possible to recite a memorized prayer without lifting up our minds and hearts to God.

Catholic schools today try to help kids learn to be aware of God's love all around and within them, and to relate to God intimately. This, they learn, is the heart of prayer. Once this foundational notion is in place, then it makes sense to teach both rote prayers and how to pray spontaneously from the heart.

As a child and teenager, my understanding of prayer was heavily conditioned by my experience of the pre–Vatican II Latin Mass, and by my experience of the many communal and private Catholic devotional activities that were popular during those years. To pray was to enter into the presence of a Profoundly Holy Mystery, a Reality beyond this world, yet in it.

Looking back on my youth as objectively as I can, it seems to me that I loved the old Latin Mass. As an eighth grader, when it was my turn I willingly rode my bicycle two miles to our parish church to serve as an altar boy at the 6 A.M. weekday Mass. To participate in the Mass and receive Holy Communion was to enter into a Mystery that literally boggled the mind. After Mass, I felt—really *felt*—renewed and refreshed in body, mind, and spirit.

Later, after the liturgical renewal launched by Vatican II gave us the Mass in English, with a priest who faced the people, sometimes I experienced a different kind of transcendence, a sense of historical transcendence. I was awed by the realization that what we were doing was so close to what the early Christians had done. I could almost imagine what it must have been like for them to celebrate the Eucharist in the first and second centuries. In more recent years, sorry to say, I became convinced that the typical parish Mass is almost terminally pedestrian, and the patient needs intensive care. I don't advocate a return to the old-style Latin Mass, but the Liturgy of the Eucharist as we find it in most parishes today reminds me of an image from T. S. Eliot's poem, "The Love Song of J. Alfred Prufrock." It's like "a patient etherized upon a table."

What Catholic who grew up in the 1940s and '50s can forget what it was like to attend Benediction of the Blessed Sacrament? Acting as an altar boy for this devotion was second only to serving Mass, and the ultimate liturgical double whammy was for Benediction to immediately follow Mass.

The priest wore a heavily embroidered gold cope over his shoulders that hung down to his ankles. The air was filled with clouds of sweet-smelling incense. We sang hymns, sometimes in Latin: "Holy God We Praise Thy Name" and "O Salutaris Hostia." The priest ascended the altar steps, turned, and blessed us with the Host (the consecrated white wafer), temporarily housed in the center of a gold sunburst monstrance. We repeated, after the priest, a special litany: "Blessed be God. (Blessed be God.) Blessed be His holy name. (Blessed be His holy name.) . . ."

Closely related to this devotion was Exposition of the Blessed Sacrament, which could last for hours. The Host in its ornate monstrance sat atop the tabernacle, above the altar, an object of devotion and worship. People came to church to pray before the exposed Blessed Sacrament for as long as they wished, and as they arrived and departed, the garden variety genuflection, on one knee, was inappropriate. Out of respect for the visible Blessed Sacrament, proper devotional etiquette called for getting down on both knees, followed by a bow. This was called a double genuflection.

During the 1950s, Marian devotions were extremely popular. Indeed, they were rampant. No Catholic elementary or high school would let the month of May pass without a ceremonial crowning of a statue of the Blessed Mother with a wreath of flowers, preferably red roses. The teachers always chose a girl to place the wreath on the Blessed Mother's head, and to be chosen was a singular honor. We sang hymns: "Salve Regina" and "Ave Maria" were popular standards.

One of the May Marian devotions in the small Catholic elementary school I attended in northern Idaho was called the "Living Rosary." The nuns chose fifty-nine kids to stand for each bead of the rosary, plus another nine kids to represent the rosary's crucifix, and we stood in the shape of a rosary in the middle of the school gymnasium. The rest of the student body knelt in the bleachers while each kid who stood for a bead in the rosary led everyone else in a Hail Mary or whatever prayer was appropriate for the bead he or she represented. The challenge for those who formed the rosary in the middle of the gym was to listen for the voice of the kid who came before you, so you wouldn't miss your turn and make a fool of yourself.

Another big influence on my spirituality from my earliest days in a Catholic school was the stories I heard and read about the lives of the saints. Granted, many of these stories were more than slightly touched by Jansenism, which presupposed that the human body, with its emotions, appetites, and sexuality, was dangerous to one's eternal destiny. All the same, these stories inspired me and gave me ideals.

I learned about the heroics of saints—St. Francis Xavier, the sixteenth-century Jesuit missionary to China, St. Teresa of Avila and St. John of the Cross, the sixteenth-century Carmelite mystics and reformers, St. John Bosco, the nineteenth-century Italian friend to poor and homeless boys, St. John Vianney, the nineteenth-century French priest who was so popular as a confessor that people knocked over his confessional in their enthusiasm, and St. Thérèse of Lisieux, the young nineteenth-century French Carmelite nun who lived and died in obscurity but became world famous.

St. Francis of Assisi was a favorite, and along with countless other Catholic kids I thought the story about St. Francis and the wolf of Gubbio was great. So important were the saints that when we went to church, statues of saints stood about to remind us of their stories. Catholic churches were loaded with visual aids, you might say.

One of the most important lessons I learned from reading and hearing the lives of the saints was that a happy life requires discipline. The saints were heroic when it came to embracing celibacy, fasting, living in poverty, spending hours in prayer, dying for the faith, and so forth. A person must make choices, you can't have everything, and sometimes it's good to voluntarily go without. Saints were people who made great sacrifices for the love of God and neighbor, and God wanted me to follow their example.

With the Second Vatican Council came a revolution in many Catholics' understanding of and attitude toward prayer and spirituality. The old devotions seemed to disappear in the wink of an eye. A new emphasis emerged on reading and praying with Scripture. Social awareness and political involvement surfaced among Catholics. The civil rights movement of the 1960s caused many Catholics to reexamine the meaning of prayer and spirituality.

At the same time, authors such as Thomas Merton, the famous Trappist monk, wrote about contemplative prayer and the benefits to be gained from learning about Eastern religious traditions, especially Zen.

From 1964 to 1968, I did time in the U.S. Navy. Following boot camp in San Diego, California, I took up space on naval air stations in Texas, Tennessee, Hawaii, and Virginia. I noticed the changes happening in the Mass, of course, the gradual switch from Latin to English, but these changes were almost incidental for me. My spirituality and approach to prayer remained the same. I took long walks after dark around the naval air station in Norfolk, Virginia, during my last months in the navy. I held my rosary inside the pocket of my heavy pea coat and prayed as I walked.

Following my discharge in August of 1968, in some ways I found myself in a church I didn't recognize. Attending classes at Santa Clara University, a Jesuit institution in California, I couldn't help but notice that the church I knew in high school, four year earlier, was quite different from the church I found now. One of the first things to go was the rosary. No one did *that* anymore.

Years later, married and the father of three sons, I rediscovered the rosary. The editor of a national Catholic newspaper asked me to write a series on prayer, and by the time I finished I realized that my own prayer life needed attention. Yet I also realized that life with three young children was not conducive to the silence and contemplative prayer I had enjoyed in college. I had heard charges, years before, that the rosary was for uneducated, simple-minded people. As I searched through a trunk full of old stuff of mine in the basement of our home, I thought, "Well, it may be for simple-minded people, but it's the best I can do right now." I began to take a two-mile walk each evening, after our children were in bed, the rosary beads slipping one by one through my fingers inside my coat pocket.

Gradually, I learned from experience that there is nothing simple-minded about the rosary at all. It is a prayer tradition with a rich past, and praying the rosary can be a thoroughly contemplative experience—it is also an excellent way for men and women to weave feminine images of God into their spirituality. To this day the rosary is one of my favorite pathways to prayer.

During my freshman year in college, I majored in English. Here's a good one on me, the future writer: The professor who taught the freshman composition course returned the first essay I handed in with a note on it scrawled in red ink: "I think I spent more time on this than you did." I was mortified beyond words.

At the beginning of my sophomore year, I changed my major to Religious Studies. This put me even more in the middle of the "hot issues" in the "new church." I'll never forget the first time I received communion in my hand, instead of on my tongue. As the farmer father of a friend of mine was fond of saying: "I like t' fell over." This was something only a priest had been allowed to do for who knew how many centuries, and here I was holding the consecrated bread in my hand, the Body of Christ! That just about knocked me out.

Strange, sometimes bizarre things happened during these years. Stories circulated of priests saying Mass in people's homes using Pepsi and Oreos instead of bread and wine. I personally witnessed a Mass in somebody's apartment where the priest used wine and tortilla chips. I volunteered to help out when a Catholic high school had not a retreat but an "advance." Priests and nuns cast off their traditional clerical or religious garb and went about in ordinary clothing.

Seattle University, another Jesuit school, had, and still has, a summer graduate program called SUMORE (Seattle University Master's of Religious Education). A friend enrolled and came back humming a new song, to the tune of a popular song from the '50s: "When you walk in the sun with a cute little nun / That's SU-MORE-AY! / When you climb Mount Rainier with a six pack of beer / That's SU-MORE-AY!"

Today's SUMORE is a perfectly fine program, with far more lay Catholics than priests and nuns enrolled. But in those days it, and many similar programs, attracted hundreds of young to middle-aged priests and nuns who seemed to be going through a delayed adolescence, and many wild and crazy things happened as a result. . . .

To say the least, my prayer life went through a period of change. I wandered into—and soon out of—the early Charismatic Renewal. Catholics gathered in huge groups on college campuses and behaved very like fundamentalist pentecostals. There was much reading aloud from the Bible and much singing of mesmerizing songs while swaying with hands raised in the air. There was much crying of, "Yes, Jee-zus!" and "Praise Jee-zus!"

People "prayed over" one another at a terrific rate per prayer meeting, hoping for "the baptism of the Holy Spirit," which sometimes resulted in tremendous emotional outbursts. People "prayed in tongues" and stood up to give "prophecies." Now and then, after being "prayed over," someone was apparently cured of some dread or not so dread physical or emotional affliction. All this was done in perfect sincerity, of course; in fact, the whole phenomenon was absolutely *awash* in sincerity.

This definitely was not what I had learned in Catholic schools. But there it was, all the same. In quieter moments, I had to admit that the typical Catholic pentecostal prayer meeting qualified as "a lifting up of our minds and hearts to God." On the other hand, in its more spectacular, more enthusiastic moments it was more like a falling of the Holy Spirit on people with an almost audible crash.

After less than six months, I slipped away from the Charismatic Renewal feeling spiritually slapped around. I was uncomfortable with the anti-intellectualism I often found there. Being at the same time an avid reader of Catholic scripture scholars such as Father Raymond Brown, I had grown uncomfortable with using the Bible in what struck me as very close to a fundamentalist fashion. I wanted more depth, more silence, and a lot less pentecostal carrying on.

In 1964, the summer before I joined the navy, I had come across one of Thomas Merton's early books, *The Sign of Jonas*. That was the beginning of my exposure to Merton, and over the years he has had a deep influence on my approach to spirituality. In large part, I think what attracted me to Merton was what struck me as a continuity in his thought with what I had learned about prayer and spirituality during my childhood and adolescence in Catholic schools. I also admired Merton's use of language, his use of slang, and the poetry that surfaced in his prose. Without saying so explicitly, Merton took the old definition of prayer, "a lifting up of our hearts and minds to God," and gave it deeper meanings than it had ever had for me before.

After my brief and ambivalent foray into Catholic pentecostalism, I returned to Merton with a passion. I read everything by him that I could lay my hands on, including older books such as *No Man Is An Island*, and more recent works such as *Contemplative Prayer* and *Contemplation in a World of Action*.

On the one hand, from Merton I learned the value of solitude, silence, and contemplative prayer. On the other hand, he taught me about the central place of human relationships and social responsibility in a healthy Christian spirituality. He also helped me to have more respect for Eastern religious traditions.

During my college years, in the midst of my studies, I began to give one to two hours a day to reading books on prayer and the spiritual life, and to a contemplative form of prayer. My prayer method, if you will, was simple. I followed Merton's suggestion to sit still, close my eyes, and repeat over and over, in unison with my breathing, a line from one of the Psalms. One of my favorites was the first verse from the New American Bible translation of Psalm 63: "O God, you are my God whom I seek. For you my flesh pines and my soul thirsts, like the earth, parched, lifeless, and without water." During some of my prayer time each day, I also read meditatively from the Bible.

Being a Religious Studies major in college couldn't help but have an impact on my understanding of prayer and spirituality. I was fortunate to study theologians such as Karl Rahner and Paul Tillich. We read works by the great Romanian historian of religion, Mircea Eliade, and long before he came to the attention of an adoring public via television interviews with Bill Moyers, my fellow students and I read Joseph Campbell's *The Hero with a Thousand Faces*. We also pondered *Man and His Symbols*, still a first-rate introduction to the thought of psychologist Carl Jung. Campbell and Jung helped me to gain a deeper, more sophisticated, more mature understanding of the sacraments and of the Bible.

From Mircea Eliade and Joseph Campbell I learned that a story doesn't have to be historical to carry truth. A myth can communicate more truth than the daily newspaper. From C. G. Jung and Paul Tillich, I learned that to call a sacrament a symbol is high praise, because it is only through a living symbol that humans can commune with God. A symbol is a human reality that opens up, reveals, and communicates the sacred for us. A myth does the same in narrative form.

From Joseph Campbell in particular, I learned how dependent we are on metaphors. Without metaphors for God, we have no way to talk about or relate to God. "Father" is a powerful Christian metaphor for God, as are "Lord," "King," and "Son of God." Some medieval mystics used feminine metaphors for God. Julian of Norwich called Jesus "our Mother." Yet I also learned that a metaphor not only reveals but conceals. The best metaphor is one that does its job but simultaneously prods us along toward the incomprehensible Divine Mystery.

More influential than any other single thinker was Karl Rahner. From studying Rahner I gained a deeper sensitivity to God's presence in the world and his working through human cultures and societies. Rahner and Merton, in fact, have so many similar themes in their respective ways of thinking that repeatedly I identified what I read by one with something I had read by the other. Both have a profound sensitivity to God's presence in human beings and in human relationships. Rahner once said that if he had to sum up all that he had written he would say, "God lives in you."

Flipping through the pages of an old copy of the *Baltimore Catechism,* I find that the authors of the catechism did believe it was important to offer some biblical perspectives. Following the question and answer on prayer, for example, the catechism quoted one verse from the Old Testament (Lam 3:41) and five from the New Testament (Mt 26:41, Lk 18:1, Jn 4:21–24, Jn 16:24, and 1 Pt 4:7).

Still, my Catholic school teachers didn't exactly urge us to turn to the Bible to see what it might say about prayer, or anything else, for that matter. They didn't attribute much importance to the Bible, which had been typical of Catholicism since the Protestant Reformation in the sixteenth century. Part of the Counter-Reformation was to downplay the Bible and emphasize the seven sacraments, because Protestants emphasized the Bible and threw out most of the sacraments.

During my college years, I got to know the Hebrew and Christian Scriptures better. I took courses on the Gospels and on Pauline theology. The professor who taught the undergraduate Old Testament course I took was a rabbi. Later, completing work for a master's degree in theology at Marquette University, I gulped down even more biblical studies, never becoming an expert but always gaining a deeper appreciation for the scriptures.

The Jerusalem Bible had been published in 1966, and it had a tremendous impact on me, as it did for many Catholics following the Second Vatican Council. Some years later, people began to realize that *The Jerusalem Bible* had its drawbacks, since it was translated from the original French version (*Bible de Jerusalem*), rather than directly from the original Hebrew and Greek texts. Still, it was a watershed version of the Bible for its time. The various introductions and footnotes were first-rate, and they helped me to understand and pray with the Bible, which I had never done before. For me, it was like a great awakening.

Prior to about the age of twenty-three, I had never read the Bible. It simply was not part of a Catholic kid's experience during the 1950s and '60s. In the fourth grade, my whole class had a text book with a title like *Old Testament History*, or some such thing, but that was just some pious Catholic author's retelling of various Old Testament stories. It was probably as fundamentalist as could be.

Readings from the Old and New Testaments were part of the Mass, but "everyone knew" they weren't all that important. I don't remember priests spending much time elaborating on the readings from Scripture during their sermons. The truth is that the average parish priest knew little about the Bible. Seminaries at the time were not long on Bible scholarship, to say the least.

When I began to study the Bible and use it as a basis for prayerful reflection during my college years, a new world opened up for me. I was nearly overwhelmed as I slowly read through the high priestly prayer of Jesus in Chapter 17 of John's Gospel. The first time I read the parable of the last judgment in Matthew 25, I was stunned. Paul's hymn about the servant Christ, in Philippians 2:5–11, floored me. "So," I remember thinking, "this is what the Christian life is all about."

I devoured the Bible almost whole, and I even completed a directed reading course in New Testament Greek. When I needed to write a paper for a class entitled, "A Theology of Alienation," the topic I chose was "Alienation and Freedom in the Judeo-Christian Tradition." During my senior year, that paper became the first article I ever had published, in a little Catholic magazine called *The Bible Today*. When a check for $30 came in the mail, I was ecstatic. I went out and bought a copy of the *Jerome Biblical Commentary*.

One direction my studies took that had a special impact on my spirituality was my attempt to follow the theme of Jesus as a man of prayer. If Jesus shows us what it means to live our humanity to its fullest, I reflected, then what better example of the place prayer should have in the lives of Christians?

Tracking down places in the Gospels where the evangelist-redactors connected Jesus and prayer, I discovered that often they included a particular gesture or posture in their descriptions. Mark, for example, the first gospel written, describes Jesus as "looking up to heaven" when he prayed for the healing of a deaf man (7:34). John describes a similar gesture ("Jesus looked upward") in his account of the raising of Lazarus from the dead (11:41).

When Luke describes Jesus at prayer in the Garden of Gethsemane, he says that Jesus "knelt down" (22:41). In Matthew's account, Jesus "threw himself on the ground" (26:39).

It was the rare instance, I knew, when a Gospel includes merely extraneous information. Therefore, when the Gospels go to the trouble to mention Jesus' posture or gestures during prayer, that has theological significance. Prayer, I concluded, is not just a spiritual act but a bodily act, as well. In Rahnerian terms, because we are "embodied spirits" prayer is at once a bodily and spiritual act.

When the old catechism defined prayer as "a lifting up of our minds and hearts to God," it was accurate as far as it went. But prayer is not just an interior act; the body needs to get involved in prayer, as well. With all the kneeling, standing, and sitting Catholics did and still do to a lesser extent during Mass, you would think this would be obvious, but it wasn't. I welcomed the Gospels' support for including the body in prayer.

It seemed then, and it still seems today, significant that in Luke's account of the occasion when Jesus taught his disciples the Our Father, Jesus prayed immediately prior to doing so (Lk 11:1–4). Ever since then, before I write about prayer, or speak about prayer, I take at least a moment to pray first myself.

Ever since my college years, I have been deeply touched by Jesus' explicit instruction to his disciples to pray in solitude: "Whenever you pray, go into your room and shut the door and pray to your Father who is in secret; and your Father who sees in secret will reward you" (Mt 6:6).

As attuned as Catholics are to communal liturgical prayer, I find to this day that without regular times for solitary prayer and reflection, my experience of the Mass loses something. So important is solitude to me that for years now I have made an annual week-long retreat at a Trappist monastery where I can soak up prayerful silence and solitude like a sponge.

In the late 1980s, praying with others became a priority for me, as well, so I polled the other members of the small faith community good spouse and I belong to and found plenty of interest in organizing a monthly prayer gathering. One evening each month we get together in a different family's home for prayer, social interaction, and snacks. The heart of our shared prayer is a modified version of the rosary.

Once everyone is present, the host couple lights candles, turns off or dims the electric lights, and introduces a theme they chose for that particular gathering. Since everyone in our small faith community is active in ministry to engaged couples, we tend to focus on various issues that relate to marriage and family life, although it's not uncommon for a host-couple to choose a theme that relates to a liturgical or calendar season.

Once the host-couple introduces the theme for the evening, they may play some appropriate recorded music, to help get us into a prayerful spirit. Some like to begin with a reading from the Bible or from a favorite book. Once the music or reading is over, the host-couple begins the rosary, and a different person leads each decade, beginning by mentioning a particular intention for that decade. Ordinarily, we don't use the traditional Sorrowful, Joyful, and Glorious mysteries. Sometimes we use a scriptural version of the rosary, prefacing each Hail Mary with an appropriate verse from Scripture.

Silence, too, has a part in our shared prayer. Between each decade, we pause in prayerful silence for two or three minutes, until another person volunteers to lead the next decade. I think we value these silent times as much as we do the times of spoken prayer.

Over the years, I have come to the conclusion that spirituality can be a misleading term. Down through the centuries, heresies that would divide soul and body, that would pit spirit against flesh, have had a long-lasting impact on Christians, and one result is an opposition between spirituality and ordinary everyday life. Thus, many people act as if spirituality relates only to "spiritual" activities: prayer, liturgy, going on retreats, and disciplines such as fasting and reading the Bible.

In the early years after I married and became a father, one of the first issues I had to deal with was how to interpret in the context of family life the traditional ideas about spirituality that I had learned as a single person. In essence, I finally decided that spirituality is close in meaning to lifestyle. My spirituality is nothing more, nor less, than the everyday ways that I try to express in my life the spirit of the gospel and the spirit of the living Catholic tradition.

My spirituality relates to how I approach all aspects of life. Spirituality relates to prayer, of course. But it also has every-thing to do with my marriage, my role as a father, and my work. An authentically Christian spirituality leads one to approach marriage, parenting, and work not just as "things I do" that are incidental to my faith. Rather, these are ways in which God has called me, and continues to call me every day, to serve him and to serve the world. My work, my family commitments, and my leisure pursuits are ways of being for God and neighbor.

A Christian spirituality is, I believe, shaped in fundamental ways by the culture in which it is lived. The dominant culture in the United States is largely consumerist in nature. That is, people draw meaning from and relate to one another in ways that support and depend upon buying, selling, and accumulat-ing material possessions and financial forms of security as ends in themselves. In our culture, there is no such thing as enough, and your very identity depends upon what you own or do not own. You have more worth as a person the more money you earn and spend, and the more affluent you become.

Given the nature of the dominant culture, an authentically Christian spirituality will, to one degree or another, be counter-cultural. At baptism, or when they embrace for themselves their baptismal commitment, Catholic Christians solemnly promise to make the love of God and neighbor the standard upon which they will base their existence. Therefore, there can't help but be a conflict between Christians and the dominant culture. A Catholic-Christian lifestyle and spirituality is automatically counter-cultural because the gospel inspires simplicity of life, not upward mobility; giving and sharing, not accumulating and stockpiling.

There's a line in a Woody Allen film, *Hannah and Her Sisters*. The character played by Woody Allen says, "If Jesus came back today and saw all the things being done in his name he would never stop throwing up." I think of this line whenever I see a statue of St. Francis of Assisi standing in the middle of a birdbath in the backyard of a big home in a very affluent neighborhood. If St. Francis came back and saw that, *he* would never stop throwing up!

At the same time, I think there are plenty of things being done in Jesus' name today that, if Jesus came back, he would be pleased to see them happening. I think of the faith and love I see in many Christian families. I think of the work done by the Missionaries of Charity, founded by Mother Teresa of Calcutta. I think of the dedication of many faith-filled people in many walks of life.

In the context of marriage and family life, I find that my spirituality can only be the spirituality of a married man, and it can only be the spirituality of a man who is a father. I express and cultivate my spirituality when I spend time with my children, when I help them to learn, and when I raise my voice to tell them to "stop doing that." I express and cultivate my spirituality when good spouse and I make love; indeed, to put it quaintly—and contrary to the persistent puritanism or Jansenism that still affects many marriages among Christians—"the pleasures of the marriage bed" are basic to a marital spirituality.

My spirituality grows and changes depending upon the ages-and-stages of my children and how long I have been married. My spirituality is different now than when our children were babies and toddlers. For one thing, I no longer have the changing of highly aromatic diapers to view as an act of sacrificial love.

My spirituality, in other words, is in large part a family spirituality. Over the years, Kathy and I discovered that in order for family prayer and rituals to have meaning, we needed to allow times for prayer and rituals to emerge from within the fabric of family life itself. Given that human life is holy because God created it, and the Son of God created it anew by becoming one of us, that means that family life is already holy. We don't need to think up ways to make it holy. Because we are a little knot of baptized but imperfect human beings sharing a life together, that means that all day and all night, every day and every night, the Holy of Holies is thick in the air.

Experience teaches us that the most significant prayer experience a family can have is also the most mundane prayer experience a family can have. Indeed, this prayer time is the holiest prayer time for a family precisely because it is the most ordinary prayer time. I'm talking about the family meal time.

Sharing a meal is a holy experience for a family. Yes, I know, family meal time can be, and often is, a time filled with conflict, no matter what the ages of the children involved. All the same, a family's meal time is a tremendously holy time. It is holy because a group of people who are trying to love one another get together to share a meal. Period. This is a time for relating to one another—even if some of that "relating" includes conflict—and that makes it a holy time. I believe that it is a big mistake to avoid conflict at meal time by figuring out a way for the family to watch TV while eating.

Family meal time is an ideal time for family prayers and rituals, right in the middle of family chaos. In our family, before we begin our evening meal together we light a candle in the middle of the table, we join hands, and we either share a moment of silent prayer or we sing a snatch of some religious song and speak our brief petitions and thank-you-Gods. And that's enough. Indeed, in today's busy-busy world, that's a whale of a lot!

Family meal time is also the ideal time for brief rituals to mark the daily passing of the liturgical seasons, Advent, Christmas, Lent, and Easter. Our Advent wreath sits smack in the middle of our table, and even as our children have gotten older they insist on opening, each day, the windows on our Advent calendar.

During Lent, on our table we place a special cross with candles on it for each week of the liturgical season that celebrates our need for ongoing conversion. Also during Lent, each evening each person gets a small pretzel on his or her plate, a traditional Lenten symbol that's edible. The shape of the pretzel represents arms crossed over chest in prayer, a posture common in the Middle Ages.

Special foods are a must at our house for Easter, and good spouse always makes a butter lamb as a symbol of the risen Christ. She also always scatters dried chopped parsley on the plate around the lamb, which drives me wild. I don't like parsley in the butter I spread on my Easter cinnamon roll!

The simple definition of prayer that I memorized from the catechism as a child started me on a pilgrimage, a journey of prayer that continues today. As my life grows and changes, my prayer and spirituality grow and change. I have the Catholic schools and institutions of higher learning that I attended to thank for giving me the foundation, and the inspiration, that keep me coming back, time after time, to start over as the beginner at prayer that I still am today.

Six

Everybody Has a Vocation

One of the first events I remember from my earliest days in a Catholic school was a visit from the pastor of our parish. Father Thomas Lafey was a smiling priest with dark, sparkling eyes framed by black hair and heavy black eyebrows. If he had let his beard grow, it would have been equally thick and black. As it was, he always seemed to have a four o'clock shadow. He knocked politely on the classroom door, Sister Angelica glanced up from her desk, stood and said, "Please come in, Father."

We children, upon hearing who it was, immediately rose from our desks and stood until Father Lafey said, "Please be seated, children." He asked Sister Angelica what we had been studying when he "so rudely" (said with a smile) interrupted us. As a matter of fact, we had been going over our catechism lesson for the day, she said.

In the course of his discussion with us—a group of squirmy third-, fourth- and fifth-graders, all in one room!— Father Lafey asked how many of the boys were going to be priests when we grew up. Most of the boys, me included, raised their hands as high as they could, and I wasn't even a Catholic yet. It would, after all, be a great honor to become a priest. How many of the girls were going to become nuns? Every girl in the room raised her hand enthusiastically.

People sometimes criticize the Catholic schools of years ago for little exercises like this, giving the impression that the only great vocations were to become priests or nuns. There is some validity to this criticism. Prior to the Second Vatican Council there was a "good, better, best" attitude in vogue in the church when it came to callings in life. It was good to be married and raise children. It was better to join a religious order or congregation and become a religious sister or brother. It was best to become a priest, the highest vocation of all.

In later years, I learned the story behind all this. The hierarchical attitude toward vocations that was common prior to Vatican II originated early in the church's history. In 312 A.D., the Roman emperor Constantine decriminalized Christianity. Sixty-eight years later, in 380 A.D., Constantine's successor, Theodosius, made Christianity the official religion of the Roman Empire, and that settled that. Clerics now had official status with the state and numerous privileges. This led to a virtual caste system in the church with bishops and priests at the top and laity at the bottom.

There was a parallel development. With Christianity no longer a crime, but the official state religion, it was no risk to embrace the faith. Before, to accept baptism was to accept the very real possibility of being thrown to the lions. Prior to Constantine, persecuting Christians had almost become a national pastime. Now, with everybody becoming a Christian, many people sought baptism because it was the in thing to do. You might have a tough time getting a job if you weren't a Christian, and if you belonged to the upper crust of society you could forget being invited to the right parties if you clung to the old gods.

Those for whom the Christian faith was more than a cultural accretion continued to take their faith seriously. They decided that since it was no longer an option to die a martyr's death for one's faith, a good substitute would be to live a celibate life of prayer and fasting out in the deserts of Egypt and Syria. We call the people who did this the desert fathers and mothers.

To make a long story short, ultimately this movement grew into monasticism in both the Eastern (Orthodox) and Western (Roman) churches. Now the way to be a truly outstanding Christian was to enter a monastery and become a monk or nun. This left those who stayed "in the world" and married with a second-class status.

In other words, developments in both church and state gave priests and both male and female religious a status superior to that of lay Christians who married and had families. Subsequent church councils, particularly the Council of Trent (1545–1563) in its reaction to the Protestant Reformation, further institutionalized the "good, better, best" system.

This was the church those of us who attended Catholic schools from the 1930s through the early '60s knew, like a fish knows the water it swims in. It was simply a given, something we did not question. We lived in a Catholic subculture that shaped our entire outlook on life and the world, and if you wanted to shine, to stand out, in that culture you became a priest, a sister, or a brother.

Question 455 in the *Baltimore Catechism* asked, "Why should Catholics show reverence and honor to the priest?" Answer: "Catholics should show reverence and honor to the priest because he is the representative of Christ Himself and the dispenser of His mysteries."

Question 197 asked, "What does Our Saviour especially recommend that is not strictly commanded by the law of God?" Answer: "Our Saviour especially recommends the observance of the Evangelical Counsels—voluntary poverty, perpetual chastity, and perfect obedience."

The catechism's commentary on this answer included the following: "The Evangelical Counsels are the most perfect of the many counsels recommended in the Gospel; they remove impediments to sanctity and are positive helps to greater holiness. . . . . The obligations of the Evangelical Counsels are assumed by the vows of the religious life, which is called the life of perfection. Those who make these vows do not thereby become perfect but they assume the obligation of tending toward perfection in a special way."

When it came to marriage, the old catechism had no such exalted language. Question 457 asked, "What is the sacrament of matrimony?" Answer: "Matrimony is the sacrament by which a baptized man and a baptized woman bind themselves for life in a lawful marriage and receive the grace to discharge their duties."

In brief, even clipped, language the catechism commented further on marriage, but only in terms of its obligations and duties, which were to "be faithful to each other" and "provide in every way for the welfare of the children God may give them." The catechism said nothing about the positive value of married couples in the church, or about marriage as a path to holiness. It acknowledged that marriage is a sacrament. Still, married couples left themselves wide open to all those "impediments to sanctity" priests and religious so wisely sidestepped.

People sometimes glance back at that period in Catholic history and look down their noses at the way things were then. They even recall with scorn the long black line of distinctively attired priests, nuns, and brothers who staffed the Catholic schools of those days. I think that is an unkind and unjust thing to do.

By the mid-1960s, it's true, the understanding of faith and of the church that had filled seminaries and religious orders and congregations with huge numbers of nuns, brothers, and priests started to come unraveled because the world was changing and, therefore, the church was changing. But the thousands of men and women who believed in that system in their youth and gave their lives to God and neighbor in the Catholic schools that contributed so much to the church and to American society during the first half of the twentieth century were, as a group, a courageous, faith-filled people to whom we owe an enormous debt of gratitude.

Still, things were changing. A major international cultural revolution began in the mid-1960s that had big-time theological implications. A church council suggested new ways to think about the church and the world. In November of 1964, the Second Vatican Council published its *Dogmatic Constitution on the Church.* This document both reflected and supported growing egalitarian convictions among Catholics.

"In the Church not everyone marches along the same path," the Council said, "yet all are called to sanctity and have obtained an equal privilege of faith through the justice of God. Although by Christ's will some are established as teachers, dispensers of the mysteries and pastors for the others, there remains, nevertheless, a true equality between all with regard to the dignity and to the activity which is common to all the faithful in the building up of the Body of Christ" (art. 32).

Exactly one year later, in November of 1965, the Council issued its *Decree on the Apostolate of Lay People.* This document declared that laity are called to holiness every bit as much as those in the priesthood or religious life. In particular, for the first time in some five hundred years the Council called the attention of Catholics to the holiness of marriage and family life.

"The Creator of all made the married state the beginning and foundation of human society," the council said; "by his grace he has made it too a great mystery in Christ and in the Church . . . and so the apostolate of married persons and of families has a special importance for both Church and civil society" (art. 11).

This was a far cry from what every Catholic school kid learned from the *Baltimore Catechism* not so many years before.

In the wake of the Second Vatican Council, priests, nuns and brothers by the thousands discerned, typically through a process that included much soul-searching and anguish, that they no longer belonged in the vocations where they had once thought they would spend their entire lives. A great deal of flailing about went on regarding vocations during the late 1960s, through the 1970s and '80s. This left the church with the present dearth of priests and religious, and where this will lead it is impossible to say.

If one thing became clear to me, it was that Christ sends all Christians, regardless of specific vocation, by virtue of their baptism, into the world to live their faith in spirit and in truth. All of us, whether lay or cleric, married, single, or vowed religious, take our basic identity from our baptism; any further commitments build on that. Further, to insist that any particular vocation makes certain persons in the church inherently superior to other persons is self-defeating.

As time passed, I gained a deeper appreciation for a scriptural perspective on fundamental life callings. The New Testament takes for granted that everyone is called to be a disciple of Jesus. The term disciple carries the twin meanings of student and follower, and all the baptized receive the fundamental call to Christian discipleship, to follow Christ no matter the specific focus or direction their life may take.

The term disciple (Greek, *mathētēs*) pops up with remarkable regularity in the New Testament, more than two hundred times. Most often, this term refers to the disciples of Jesus, but in many cases the evangelist-redactors meant references to Jesus' disciples to refer to those who heard or read their writings, as well. When we read in the Gospels, therefore, that Jesus called his disciples in such-and-such a manner, or taught his disciples this or that, in some way these words apply as much to us as they did to Jesus' original disciples.

Mark, the oldest Gospel, makes it clear that the call to Christian discipleship takes priority over secondary vocations, including the work we do. "As Jesus passed along the Sea of Galilee," Mark says, "he saw Simon and his brother Andrew casting a net into the sea—for they were fishermen. And Jesus said to them, 'Follow me and I will make you fish for people.' And immediately they left their nets and followed him. As he went a little further he saw James son of Zebedee and his brother John, who were in their boat mending nets. Immediately he called them; and they left their father Zebedee in the boat with the hired men, and followed him" (1:16–20).

Mark's Gospel does not intend this to be a mere historical recollection but an illustration of how we, too, should view our faith relationship with the risen Christ. He calls us, and we are challenged to put our Christian discipleship second to nothing.

The Gospel of Matthew adds further to our understanding of discipleship when it insists that even family ties take a back seat. "Whoever loves father or mother more than me," Matthew's Jesus says, "is not worthy of me; and whoever loves son or daughter more than me is not worthy of me. . . ." (10:37).

Matthew's original audience, in the mid-80s A.D., included many converts and potential converts to Christianity who had to take such words literally. It was not unlikely that unbelieving family members would disown or ostracize them once they embraced Christianity. This is not as much of a likelihood for people today, but the point remains valid. If push comes to shove, the baptismal commitment to Christian discipleship takes priority even over family relationships.

Granted, Matthew's Gospel says, this will be difficult. But we must expect discipleship to bring the cross in one form or another: "Whoever does not take up the cross and follow me is not worthy of me" (10:38). The life of the disciple of Christ mirrors, even embodies, the mystery at the heart of Jesus' own life: "Those who find their life will lose it, and those who lose their life for my sake will find it" (10:39).

The Gospel of Luke (10:1–20) makes it even more clear that Jesus' teachings on discipleship apply to all of his followers. In Luke, Jesus directs his words not just to "the Twelve," but to all seventy of the disciples he sends "to every town and place where he himself intended to go." Jesus declares that we should not expect discipleship to be a picnic. Rather, he sends us out "like lambs into the midst of wolves." In spite of the risks, we are not to worry about our personal safety. "Carry no purse, no bag, no sandals. . . ." Instead, we are to fly by the seat of our pants.

What are we to do on this mission of discipleship? The assignment remains the same down through the ages, to "cure the sick" and announce the nearness of the kingdom of God. We may take this as a reference to the countless kinds of "sickness" in the world: physical, emotional, psychological, and spiritual.

We are to be healers in whatever manner we are able. Most of us will bring healing to our world not by attending medical, nursing, or dental school and then by going to serve the poor in a Third World nation. Most of us will heal by dedicating ourselves, from the roots of our existence, to active love for God and neighbor. That way, no matter what we do specifically with our days and weeks, we will bring a healing spirit into the lives of others.

To proclaim the kingdom of God means, most fundamentally, living a life full of hope, joy, and active love for others. We live in a culture where many people use artificial stimulants to get an artificial sense of well-being. We can proclaim the kingdom of God by trying to live simply and by cultivating a healthy family life, good friends, and loving intimacy with the Divine Mystery at the heart of our existence. Such a life will give witness that human and divine love is a wellspring of hope, joy, and fulfillment.

Those who accept the invitation to Christian discipleship—which is an ongoing experience of the cross and resurrection of Christ—should rejoice, Luke's Jesus says, because "your names are written in heaven."

Discipleship—following Christ and learning from him—is foundational, it is the bottom line of a Christian life. Everything else can and does change in the course of a lifetime, but discipleship does not. Discipleship inspires, shapes, and directs everything else that we do.

If I am married, my discipleship shapes and guides my marriage and family life. If I discern a call to serve the people of God as a priest or as a member of a religious order or congregation, my discipleship undergirds and forms this calling. If, willingly or unwillingly, I find myself called to live as a single person, my single life will, if I am open to this, be filled with a powerful sense of Christian discipleship.

Sometimes people discover that their commitment to discipleship can lead them from one way of life to another. A friend of mine tells a story that illustrates what I mean.

My friend attended Catholic schools, and as he began his studies at a Catholic university he felt a deep longing to give his entire life to Christ. He felt no desire to become a priest, so after his sophomore year in college he joined a congregation of religious brothers that taught in Catholic elementary and secondary schools. With a deep interest in regular communal and personal prayer, my friend looked forward to his six months as a candidate and his year as a novice. "I enjoyed this time and got a lot out of it," he told me. "But later, after I went to live in a community at a high school near the university I was to attend, things began to sour."

This was during the late 1960s, and religious communities were going through major changes, with many people leaving. After one year as a novice, living in a rural quasi-monastic setting, my friend found the community he was sent to little more than "a group of bachelors living in the same residence."

Most of the traditional structures of religious life were gone—the rigidly structured times for prayer, silence, and community recreation, for example—and for understandable reasons. The old structures no longer fit, but there was no agreement on new ones, either. Few wore the traditional religious habit anymore; instead, they dressed in ordinary clothing, some quite fashionably. The brothers lived a comfortable life, my friend said, and they ate beautifully prepared meals. But there was no community life to speak of, and as time went by, fewer and fewer brothers attended the community's morning and evening prayer-times and morning Mass.

"During the time that I lived in that community," my friend said, "I spent a lot of time in prayer, and I read a lot about Scripture and the theology of the vows of poverty, chastity and obedience. What I saw being lived there—and in the other communities of brothers who belonged to that congregation—didn't make sense. It seemed like all you had to do was agree to be celibate, and a life of comfort, security, and even luxury was handed to you on a silver platter. I couldn't believe it, and I was very disappointed."

My friend began to look for alternatives. He investigated more traditional monastic communities, but they didn't seem right for him. Eventually, he left the religious congregation he had joined and returned to school on his own, all the while clinging to his sense of Christian discipleship. Where, he wondered, could he live a life that would not protect him from the risks that he believed authentic discipleship should entail? How could he live a Catholic-Christian life where he would need to depend on his faith in real, tangible ways?

Before long, my friend met a young woman. He was astounded to meet a woman who shared not only his Catholic roots and traditions, but his dedication to a life of Christian discipleship. "It was incredible," he recalled. "We were both surprised to meet someone who was not pietistic but who wanted first of all to follow Christ and live a life based on faith."

My friend and his newfound "soul-mate" reflected together on what it would mean to bring their dedication to Christian discipleship to marriage and family life. There would be insecurity, that was for sure, plenty of opportunities to trust in God, many opportunities to accept the will of God in everything from becoming parents to believing in God's care for them in the midst of financial concerns.

The young man and woman decided to marry, and their witness to a life of Christian discipleship began immediately. They wanted nothing to do with a high-priced wedding, so she made her own wedding dress and, this being the early '70s, his peasant-style wedding shirt. The wedding itself took place in a university student chapel that had no pews. This made it easy to have a reception in the same room, immediately following the wedding Mass. Instead of wedding presents, friends and family contributed decorations, snacks, and refreshments for the wedding and reception.

"All along," my friend said, "I had wanted a way of life that would allow me to live my faith in ways that would not be just talk, in ways that would allow me to struggle to be a disciple of Christ in the real world. Growing up Catholic, I had always thought that becoming a priest or religious was the best way to do this. Little did I know that becoming an 'ordinary married person' would turn out to be a much better way, for us, at least."

Indeed, most people are called to live out their Christian discipleship in marriage and family life. This calling demands tremendous faith and trust in God.

As the years have gone by, my own experience of marriage and parenthood have led me to certain convictions about the meaning of Christian discipleship in marriage and family life. Most basically, I believe that anything we read in the New Testament, or anything that we learn from the living stream of Christian tradition, including the official teachings of the church, can and should have meaning in the context of marriage and family life.

Let's take a scriptural example. A major New Testament theme declares that love of God and neighbor is the heart of the matter. In the Gospel of Mark, a scribe asks Jesus, "Which commandment is the first of all?" Jesus answers, "The first is, 'Hear, O Israel: the Lord our God, the Lord is one; you shall love the Lord your God with all your heart, and with all your soul, and with all your mind, and with all your strength.' The second is this, 'You shall love your neighbor as yourself.' There is no other commandment greater than these" (12:28–31).

If my conviction holds water, then this central gospel theme should have meaning in the context of marriage and family life, and it does. Married people and parents are called to love God with all their being as all Christians are. But spouses and parents are called to seek loving intimacy with God precisely by means of the circumstances of their life. Mark's Jesus does not say we are commanded to love "people," but, rather, our "neighbor," which means those closest to us. For married people that means the spouse, and for parents that means their children.

We live the heart of our Christian discipleship by loving God and neighbor not as people in monasteries do, but in the ways available to us in marriage and family life. The Gospel of Matthew sheds more light on this issue. In Matthew's version of the story, Jesus puts an additional spin on the twin commandments to love God and neighbor. First Matthew's Jesus says that we are to "love the Lord your God with all your heart, and with all your soul, and with all your mind." But then Jesus says that the second commandment, to love our neighbor, is "like" the first (22:37–39). In other words, the second commandment is *equal to* or *the same as* the first."

Karl Rahner, probably the greatest Catholic theologian of the twentieth century, declared that love of God and neighbor are profoundly related to each other. "Only one who loves his or her neighbor can know who God actually is," Rahner said. "And only one who ultimately loves God . . . can manage unconditionally to abandon himself or herself to another person, and not make that person the means of his or her own self-assertion."

In marriage and family life, Christian discipleship inspires a love for God that most often shows itself in an active, loving service of one another. But Christian discipleship also inspires forms of prayer and ritual that are appropriate to marriage and family life.

Husband and wife come to "know who God actually is" through each other and through their children, whether they give birth to those children biologically or welcome them into their life through adoption. At the same time, spouses and parents love each other and their children because at the heart of their commitment to marriage and family life is a desire for loving intimacy with God to match that cultivated by the most devout Trappist monk.

" 'For this reason a man will leave his father and mother and be joined to his wife, and the two will become one flesh,' " says the Letter to the Ephesians. "This is a great mystery, and I am applying it to Christ and the church" (5:31–32).

In other words, the love between husband and wife, and the love of God which they experience in their love for each other, mirrors and makes present in the world the love Christ has for his people, the church. This is what it means to say that husband and wife give their Christian discipleship a specific shape precisely by being married and by loving and raising their children together.

That is one example of how something we read in Scripture has meaning in the context of marriage and family life. Now let's turn to an example from the living stream of Catholic-Christian tradition. One insight from sacred tradition that shaped Christian discipleship down through the centuries is the insight that to remain alive and kicking, any Christian life requires times for prayerful silence and solitude. What should this mean for husbands and wives and parents? It seems so incompatible with the hurly-burly demands of family life, especially in our culture today.

The insight that Christian discipleship requires times for prayerful silence and solitude looms large in sacred tradition, therefore it must have meaning in marriage and family life. Otherwise it does not deserve to loom large, but is only a minor strand of tradition relevant to the few.

Over the years, I learned that this tradition has more than a little relevance to marriage and family life, even if we don't hear much about it in the typical Sunday homily. If anything, our cultural context makes even more acute the need for married people and parents to have times for prayerful silence and solitude. Many Catholics are heavily indoctrinated by the mass media with the pseudo-religious gospel of consumerism, and such people need times to reflect quietly on the meaning of Christian discipleship.

No matter where they live, there are places within reach where married people can go for solitary prayer and the healing that only silence can give. Husbands and wives need encouragement from priests and other parish ministers to give each other this time away, now and then.

I know the value of times like this, because for years Kathy and I have given each other an annual one week retreat at a Trappist monastery's guest facilities. I go there for my own sake, for the sake of my marriage, and for the sake of my role as a father. I don't come back magically transformed into Superhusband or Superfather, but I come back refreshed in body, mind, and spirit. I return home with a renewed dedication to my faith and to my commitment to be a disciple of Jesus in the midst of marriage and family life.

Of course, there are other times throughout the year when good spouse and I get away for a day now and then, at a nearby house of prayer, for example. We find that times like this help us to maintain some emotional, psychological, and spiritual distance from the more absurd aspects of a consumer culture that mass media advertising campaigns promote so effectively. We find that times like this help us to maintain some focus on love of God and neighbor as our ultimate standard.

Of course, not everyone is called to live his or her Christian discipleship by being married and raising children. Some, by choice or by chance, are called to live a single life. Christian discipleship for single people can take many different forms, sometimes involving work or career, and parish and other volunteer activities in more central ways than it may for married people, parents, or priests or religious. Still, single people remain members of their extended family network, and family relationships continue to shape their discipleship in important ways.

Some men are called to become priests, and unless you happen to be a married Episcopalian priest who converted to Catholicism, this requires a commitment to celibacy. Some men and women are called to the religious life, which is also a celibate lifestyle.

As with the commitment to marriage and family life, or a single life, those who become priests, or sisters or brothers, do so as a way to give a specific form or direction to their baptismal dedication to Christian discipleship. Beyond this, there is

a great deal of uncertainty today about the ↑
about the religious life. I know what I, as a pa┆
Catholic, think the Christian discipleship of p┆
gious communities should look like, so that ⌐⌐ ⌐⌐⌐ ⌐
discuss here.

I want a priest to be a mature human being who is not inclined to authoritarianism. Just as an immature person can't have a healthy marriage, so an immature person can't be a good priest. This does not mean that a priest can't make mistakes or be imperfect. It does mean that he should be able to admit mistakes and move on from there.

The discipleship of a priest is one of service, so I want a priest to be a leader, not a dictator. Most Catholics no longer welcome the old model of the parish priest as benevolent autocrat. A priest should be comfortable working with a parish council made up of people who will not always agree with one another or with their pastor. In so far as possible, the parish priest should be less an administrator and more a pastor, teacher, and guide.

I want a priest who takes his days off, especially when he is too busy to do so. A priest who is stressed out, burned out, and frazzled is not much good to anyone. A priest should feel okay about telling the parish council that he has too many responsibilities and needs more help. There is no such thing as Superpriest.

I want a priest who can relax, drop the priestly persona and enjoy being with people. A parish priest should be as comfortable in the middle of a party or parish picnic as he is in the middle of a liturgy. A priest should be grown-up enough to relate to both women and men as equals. He should be childlike enough to relate to children with warmth, joy, and respect. Not all priests will have the gifts needed to work with teenagers, but those who do should be allowed to make youth ministry a major commitment.

I want a priest who can make decisions. Bill Gates, the youthful founder and CEO of the Microsoft Corporation, once said that he would rather make a bad decision and have to corct it later than make no decision at all. A pastor can't please all of the people all of the time, and I want a parish priest to accept this fact of life.

I want a parish priest who understands that as families go today so will go the church of the future. John Paul II insists that "family life is the very substance of parish life." Therefore, priests should make a major commitment to nourishing family life in today's parishes.

These are not easy times for priests, and I want a priest to be a person who can relax and share his troubles not only with his fellow priests but with some of us "ordinary folks" as well. A priest who remains distant from the people he is called to serve is not, in my book, a good priest.

I want a priest who is a prayerful person and familiar with the ways of the spiritual life as it must be lived in the real world. I am not crazy about priests who abandon the traditional blessing at the end of the Mass. Some change it from "may almighty God bless you in the name of the Father, and of the Son, and of the Holy Spirit" to "may God bless *us* . . ." or some variation thereof. I bless my children, why shouldn't a priest bless the Eucharistic assembly? Are some priests worried that they will be perceived as too paternalistic if they do this? Fooey. That's not the kind of paternalism I object to.

I want a priest who can preside at the Eucharist without imposing his personality on the liturgy. I want a priest to preside, not perform as if he were an entertainer before an audience. Lead the assembly through the ritual words and actions of the Mass; don't do a liturgical dog-and-pony act by improvising every other thing from beginning to end.

When it comes to the priest's role as teacher and guide, he must sometimes, of necessity these days, walk a fine line between some of the church's official teachings (on birth control, for example) and the faith experience of the people he is sent to serve, listening carefully and prayerfully to both. If a priest is going to err in one direction or the other, I want him to err on the side of the people and their experience of faith.

Above all, I want a priest to be on intimate terms with the gospel. I don't expect most priests to be walking, talking saints, but I do expect a priest to recognize when the gospel should be a comfort and when it should be a challenge. I want to hear homilies that, to use the old phrase, comfort the afflicted and afflict the comfortable.

Turning to religious communities, to put it as succinctly as possible, I want them to take their vows seriously. I seem to sense much talk these days on the part of religious communities about living the spirit of their vows. I'd like to see them not use this as an excuse to throw the baby out with the bathwater.

Those who take a vow of poverty should have something in common with those who are poor through no choice of their own. They should venerate "Saint" Henry David Thoreau, who said, "Simplify, simplify. . . ." Those who take a vow of celibacy should be passionately in love with God, and their prayer life should show it. They may have more time to work on behalf of others, but I don't want religious to use that as an excuse to neglect their commitment to prayer.

Those who take a vow of obedience should have something in common with those whose very existence depends on obeying the harsh directives of the real world. I want religious to serve where they are most needed, not just where they would like to go.

The vows religious take should give direction to their Christian discipleship, and it should be a distinctive direction that is clear for all to see.

Many religious communities of men and women have been wearing ordinary clothing for many years now. After remaining open-minded about this all along, I came to the conclusion that the experiment is a failure. Most nuns look merely dowdy. A few go overboard in the other direction and try to keep up with the fashionable dress codes of the business community. Many male religious dress like nerds, although a few take the expensive route of the clotheshorse or the snappy dresser. The old-style traditional habits may have been impractical, and they may have lost their "witness value," but the new approach is no improvement.

Enough, I say. There is nothing wrong with religious dressing in ordinary clothing sometimes, but it's time to return to some form of religious habit for everyday wear. The tradition of wearing distinctive garb originated for good practical and theological reasons, I dare say, and it's time to discover what those reasons were. It's just possible that it could have something to do with embodying the spirit of the three vows that members of religious communities take.

Priests and religious dedicate themselves to Christian discipleship in ways that most Catholics do not. Therefore, they commit themselves to a spirituality and lifestyle that is supposed to compliment and be different from the spirituality and lifestyle of most Catholics.

When Father Thomas Lafey asked my third-grade class how many of us were going to be priests and nuns when we grew up, he reflected the attitudes of the time. There was this truth behind his words, however, and it is a truth that I have never forgotten: Each one of us is called by God to a particular form of Christian discipleship, a way of life that will give a specific direction to our baptismal promise to love God and neighbor above all else. It's up to us, with the grace of God, to respond to that calling faithfully and with all our heart, whatever it may be.

Seven

The Universe Is Sacramental

In a church where most people are baptized as infants, I have the distinction of being able to remember my own baptism because I was ten years old when it happened. Late on a Saturday afternoon in May, while the sun shone outside, in the little parish church of Saints Peter and Paul, my parents, my sister, and I, and our various godparents, gathered around the baptismal font. Located in the back of the church, the font was almost as tall as I was. My sister and I had to balance on a footstool when the time came for Father Lafey to pour the holy water over our foreheads. "I baptize thee in the name of the Father, and of the Son, and of the Holy Ghost," the priest said.

Immediately after we were baptized, we each made our First Confession, a sacramental progression which seems theologically preposterous today, but that's the way it was in 1956. Kneeling in the darkened confessional booth, for the first time I experienced the old sacrament of Penance, a ritual that was at once anxiety inducing and a source of tremendous relief.

The old ritual fit a legalistic popular piety for which sin was primarily a violation of moral laws. It would be years before I would learn that sin can hardly be reduced to a neat list of things I did or did not do, together with a tally of how many times for each. It would be years before I would learn that sin is far more subtle and insidious than that, more like a fundamental orientation away from God and neighbor that people struggle against all their lives.

The old laundry-list approach to sin and confession focused more on the symptoms of a sinful condition, not its substance. The old Catholic perspective on sin also put sexual sins near the top of the list, maybe just below murder, a priority the New Testament knows nothing about.

The morning after our baptism, we knelt in church during Mass, waiting for the key moment, after the priest said, "Domine non sum dignus" three times. My sister and I entered the sanctuary (O rare privilege!), knelt on the first altar step, and stuck out our tongues to receive Jesus "under the appearance of bread" for the first time.

As a Catholic school kid, I had prepared for baptism, first confession, and first communion by keeping up with the rest of my class as we memorized material from the *Baltimore Catechism*. The answers to Questions 315 through 329 explained what baptism was all about. I knew by heart that baptism was "the sacrament that gives our souls the new life of sanctifying grace by which we become children of God and heirs of heaven."

If that wasn't good news, I didn't know what was. I knew that baptism "takes away original sin; and also actual sins and all the punishment due to them," if, in fact, I was guilty of any actual sins and was "truly sorry" for them. An "actual sin" was "any willful thought, desire, word, action or omission forbidden by the law of God." I learned that baptism made me a member of "the church, subject to its laws, and capable of receiving the other sacraments."

"The law of God" and "subject to its laws." Those phrases made a big impression on my ten-year-old mind and imagination. It was critically important to know what those laws were! God's laws and the church's laws—that was where the rubber hit the road. Unfortunately, this led to a vein of legalism in my spirituality which I would live with for years. Only as a young adult did I learn that legalism is incompatible with authentic faith, that in the New Testament both Jesus and Paul reject any such perspective.

Learning about baptism, I marveled that under certain circumstances even I could baptize someone. "The priest is the usual minister of Baptism," the answer to Question 318 said, "but if there is danger that someone will die without Baptism, anyone else may and should baptize."

"May *and should* baptize . . ."! I daydreamed about coming upon some poor schnook who had just been hit by a car, lying in a pool of blood, clinging to life by a thread, begging me to baptize him. He had been such a fool not to seek baptism years ago. I would dash to a nearby house and bang on the door. "Hurry! Get me a glass of water! I have to baptize a guy before he dies!" I would hurry back, pour the water over the dying man's forehead, say the words, and just as I finished he would croak. What a hero I would be! I had saved his immortal soul!

Baptism was, the catechism said, "necessary for the salvation of all men," meaning women, too, but inclusive language was light years away. Why was baptism necessary for salvation? Because "Christ has said, 'Unless a man be born again of water and the Spirit he cannot enter into the kingdom of God.' "

Ah, but there was more to baptism than this. Things were just getting interesting. There was an escape clause. People who were not baptized could be saved if they had missed being baptized "through no fault of their own." Such a person could be saved, said the answer to Question 321, "through what is called baptism of blood or baptism of desire."

Baptism of blood! Holy mackerel! This was talk to shift a boy's imagination into overdrive. "An unbaptized person receives the baptism of blood when he suffers martyrdom for the faith of Christ."

I daydreamed about becoming a martyr. There I was, the sun hot on my face, as the executioner prepared to separate my head from my body. I would go St. Thomas More one better. Joking with the masked headsman, Thomas More asked him to spare the long beard he had grown while imprisoned in the Tower of London. The beard, More said, had done no wrong.

That was a good line, but *I* would laugh in death's face. "Ho, ho, Sir Executioner! You think you deprive me of my life! You empty-headed scoundrel, you but send me to Paradise! Strike! Tarry not! I will pray for your miserable soul before the throne of God!"

On the other hand, martyrdom did mean dying, and I was only ten years old. Besides, dying wasn't strictly necessary, since I was already baptized in the normal fashion. At the same time, why would someone who was not baptized die for "the faith of Christ"? I didn't quite understand this "baptism of blood" business, but it did have a great ring to it.

The "baptism of desire" was a different matter. "An unbaptized person receives the baptism of desire," said the answer to Question 323, "when he loves God above all things and desires to do all that is necessary for his salvation."

To be perfectly honest, I couldn't imagine such a person. How could someone love God above all things and desire to do all that is necessary for salvation without hearing about God and what was necessary for salvation from another Catholic, preferably a priest or nun? In which case, even if the information came from an ordinary Catholic the person could be baptized. I didn't get it, I really didn't get it, and I told Sister Angelica so. She gave me her look that said, "Are you trying to be a smart aleck?" then she tried to explain.

"Maybe the person heard about God and about the church after being taken a prisoner of war, or something like that," S'tr said. "And maybe no water is available."

"But . . ."

"Oh, hush, and stop being such a smarty pants."

Which I did, believe me.

As a newly baptized Catholic, I embraced The Faith enthusiastically. The chain around my neck gathered weight as one saint's medal after another added to its burden. If anyone attacked me, I could have laid open my assailant's head with one whack from that collection. I stockpiled holy cards like other kids hoarded baseball cards from packages of bubble gum.

Sitting with the rest of my class in church, exercising our vocal chords on "Mother Dear, O Pray For Me," I would gaze toward the altar and envision myself a priest. That would be the life, no need to dirty one's hands with "the things of the world." All a priest did was say Mass, hear confessions, administer the other sacraments, and visit the kids in the Catholic school. Plus, he had no wife to make him pick up his dirty socks!

My preparation for baptism took place during Lent. The late Idaho winter was unkind, but Sister Angelica was not. For a half hour after school each day during the month before Easter, we sat together in a sunny little room filled with cupboards, right next to the principal's office.

I don't recall a word Sister said. All I remember is the glow and the peace and the warmth. Sister Angelica didn't just sit in that little room with me; she became a presence there. Into that over-blown closet each school day stepped someone I had never met before, full of a quiet interest in me that felt like love.

One day Sister Angelica handed me a pocket-sized missal titled *Ave Maria*. On its imitation black leather front was a gold cross with a leafy vine climbing all over it. Inside, the Table of Movable Feasts went all the way to the impossible year of 1973. My little book presented a Catholicism of lists: The Six Commandments of the Church, Six Truths We Must Know and Believe, The Four Sins Crying to Heaven for Vengeance, Nine Ways of Being Accessory to Another's Sin (yikes!), and The Six Sins against the Holy Ghost.

Sister no doubt explained the Mass, but I don't remember. In a drawer where odds and ends congregate, I still have that small black missal. Now and then I flip through its pages and dumbly wonder where the years have gone. . . .

As our baptism and first communion days approached, my sister and I had to practice receiving the host. My sister's teacher, a young nun with a beautiful face—which was all of her we could see besides her hands, thanks to her religious habit—stood us up in the principal's office. She said that the bread she was going to place on our tongues wasn't Holy Communion. It was just for practice.

Out came a little brown cardboard box with scraps of flat, white, plastic-looking wafers in it. I would never have called it bread. Sister instructed us on how to kneel, tilt back our heads, and stick out our tongues. We went through a couple of dry runs—given the quality of the bread, *very* dry runs—but without kneeling down right there in the principal's office: head back, tongue out, wafer on tongue, tongue back in, practice swallowing without chewing.

I understand that some Catholic school nuns told their students not to chew the Host because if they did, "Jesus will bleed." I find this incredible. I suppose it happened, but the nuns who taught in the Catholic schools I attended never said any such thing. They were Pacific Northwest nuns and had more common sense, maybe, than nuns in other parts of the country.

Following baptism and First Communion, my life turned unremarkable. But if I am a Catholic today it has less to do with catechism questions and answers than with the Lent of 1956 and a Benedictine nun in a long black habit. If in later years I relish things like having ashes smudged on my forehead in the form of a cross on Ash Wednesday, saints, the pope, lighted candles, clouds of sweet-smelling incense in church, the Easter vigil, holy water in little fonts inside church doors, and bringing up my own children Catholic, I can trace it to that childhood Lent when Sister Angelica became an occasion of grace.

As a Catholic school kid, I learned about the sacraments from the catechism. But more important, I was steeped daily in a sacramental environment, one where everyone took for granted that God was in the air. It took no great leap of faith to believe that bread and wine could become the body and blood of Jesus. God was everywhere, so why couldn't Jesus be in bread and wine?

The main thing I received from the Catholic school environment—and the same is true for my children today—was a sensitivity or receptivity to the presence of the Divine Mystery in anything and everything: people, places, things, anything could reflect or manifest God at any time. This is a big part of what makes Catholics Catholic. Theologian Father David Tracy calls this "the analogical imagination," the ability to see pointers to and reflections of God, analogies for God, just about anyplace. All of creation mirrors the Divine Mystery because God is more like than unlike creation.

Protestants are more inclined to say that God is more unlike than like creation. But Catholics see God around every corner and hear rumors of God in every breeze, because they have a sacramental imagination. Water, bread, wine, art, oil, words, burning incense, stories, gestures, music, dance, candy, and ice cream, all can manifest the presence of the risen Christ because these things are holy to begin with. Reflections of God can occur in popular culture, too: movies, rock music, the World Series, works of fiction, newspaper comic strips.

Over the years, I gained a deep appreciation for the ways in which Mary, the mother of Jesus, and human sexual intimacy bring God into human experience in powerful ways. On an experiential level, I gained a new appreciation for the Blessed Mother by rediscovering the rosary, and I gained a new appreciation for God's presence in the sexual intimacy of being married.

On a cognitive level, building on my experience, I developed a deeper understanding of these two "analogies for God" by reading books by theologian David Tracy (*Blessed Rage for Order* and *The Analogical Imagination*) and by sociologist and novelist Father Andrew Greeley (including *The Great Mysteries,* a novel: *Patience of a Saint,* and *How to Save the Catholic Church,* co-authored with Mary Greeley Durkin).

The image of Mary is a feminine analogy for God. Mary reveals how like a loving mother God is. God is like the Blessed Mother, nurturing, warm, giving birth. Granted, as Greeley points out, if we carry this analogy too far we may slip into

Mariolotry—Mary worship—and this has happened. This is one reason Catholics object when anyone accuses them of "worshipping" Mary. We do not worship her, we "venerate" her, we respect and honor her. Still, God is like the Blessed Mother, who shows us dimensions of the Divine Mystery that we might not appreciate as deeply otherwise.

In recent years, I learned that Mary holds a special place in the analogical or sacramental imagination of Catholics, and the best place to discover this is in poetry and in traditional prayers and hymns. During my annual retreat at a Trappist monastery, one of the most moving moments of each day comes during Compline, or Night Prayer, when the monks sing a traditional hymn to Mary. In the darkened monastery church, all the lights are off except the one that illuminates a portrait of Our Lady of Guadalupe.

The monks kneel and, in Latin, sing the Salve Regina, which dates from the eleventh century:

> Hail, Holy Queen,
> Mother of Mercy:
> Hail, our life, our sweetness and our hope:
> To thee do we cry,
> poor banished children of Eve:
> to thee do we send up our sighs,
> mourning and weeping
> in this vale of tears.
> Turn, then, most gracious advocate,
> thine eyes of mercy toward us;
> and after this, our exile,
> show unto us the blessed fruit of thy womb, Jesus.
> O clement, O loving, O sweet Virgin Mary.

I cherish a traditional Catholic devotion to Mary. At the same time, in recent years I have grown uncomfortable with some forms of Marian devotional activity. I am not excited by the reports of Marian apparitions in a rural part of what used to be Yugoslavia, and I find the "messages" from the Blessed

Virgin that the young "visionaries" report to be harmless, at best; groundlessly apocalyptic and sensational, at worst. I cannot take seriously the report that the Blessed Virgin dictated her autobiography to one of the young "visionaries," who merely awaits the go-ahead from the Virgin to publish it.

During the years since I was a ten-year-old newly baptized Catholic, I learned that there are two extremes to avoid in devotion to Mary. Theologian Father Richard McBrien, in *Catholicism*, calls these "Marian minimalism" and "Marian maximalism." The former doesn't give Mary enough credit, the latter gives her too much credit.

Marian minimalism implies that Mary could not be a legitimate analogy for God. Marian maximalism implies that Mary herself is a divine being, or almost so. Between these two erroneous extremes, Father McBrien wrote, "there is a wide spectrum of legitimate devotional options," and we should be careful about judging in a negative fashion a Marian devotion from another culture merely because it may seem weird to us. McBrien suggests the following criteria for judging a Marian devotion, and I paraphrase:

1. Devotion to Mary and all the saints is, ultimately, devotion to Christ, for it is his grace that is victorious in their lives.
2. Jesus Christ, as both human and divine, is the only mediator between humankind and God.
3. It is also true, however, that God's grace, or self-gift, is present and comes to us through other created realities, including other persons, such as Mary, who are superlative examples of the transforming power of this grace.
4. God gives us spiritual healing and liberation ("salvation") not just as isolated individuals, but as members of a faith community which shares in God's own life. So our devotion to Mary should have a communal dimension.

5. Mary, in virtue of her deep faith and obedience to the will of God, is both a "model of the church" and a disciple of Christ par excellence. She shows the church what to be, and she shows Christians how to be.

6. As the true mother of Jesus Christ, Mary is called the "God-bearer." In this sense, Mary is a "model of the church," because the church is a "reality imbued with the hidden presence of God" (Pope Paul VI).

7. Still, the church is not the kingdom of God, even though the Second Vatican Council called it "the initial budding forth" of the kingdom (*Dogmatic Constitution on the Church*, art. 5). Just so, Mary does not mediate or "channel" Christ to us, even though she is Jesus' mother and, as such, carries the incarnate Word in her womb.

8. Above all, Mary is one of "the redeemed." That she was not touched by Original Sin does not mean that she did not need redemption. She was "full of grace" due to the redemption accomplished by Christ.

9. If one is to err with regard to Mary, it would be more orthodox to err on the side of giving Mary too little credit than in giving her too much credit. St. Thomas Aquinas worried that the doctrine of the Immaculate Conception might detract from the universal nature of the redemption accomplished by Christ.

10. When it comes to reported appearances and visions of Mary, we may either believe or disbelieve. None of these are essential to Christian faith, whether they receive the official stamp of approval from the church or not. Ultimately, for everyone except those who have such special experiences, they have no final authority whatsoever.

11. "Messages" from those who claim to have "visions" of Mary can never be put on a par with the Gospels. We must always measure such "messages" against Scripture and sacred tradition, and they must not conflict with any essential part of the Christian faith.

Personally, as times goes by I find myself returning to the "old standards" for cultivating my affection for the Blessed Mother. I pray the Memorare: "Remember, O most gracious Virgin Mary, that never was it known that anyone who fled to thy protection, implored thy help, or sought thy intercession, was left unaided. . . ." I have rediscovered the marvelous poetry of the Alma Redemptoris Mater: "O loving Mother of the Redeemer, Gate of Heaven, Star of the Sea, assist thy people who have fallen, yet strive to rise again. . . ."

The other analogy for God that I experience as a kind of sacrament is marital sexual intimacy. My biblical studies taught me that God created human sexuality and called it, along with the rest of creation, "very good" (Genesis 1:31). Men and women together reflect something of God, as Genesis says: "So God created humankind in his image, in the image of God he created them; male and female he created them" (1:27). Therefore, distortions in our understanding of human sexuality, that have had a persistent grip on the Christian spirit and imagination for centuries, are completely out of place.

Yes, human nature is "fallen," but that does not mean that our sinfulness is like a steam roller that we should throw ourselves in front of so it can squash us. Rather, we are called to resist our fallenness and strive for better things, including the healthy integration of our sexuality into our lives.

Catholic tradition insists that we are not completely "fallen," that God's self-gift in Christ, his grace, puts us well on the path to recovery, and this grace is in the process of transforming every dimension of our being, including our sexuality. Therefore, our sexuality can and should be "an occasion of grace."

In marriage, this means that when husband and wife relax, cast inhibitions to the wind, get romantic, and make love, the more pleasure they experience the more graced their lovemaking is. Granted, in a normal marriage if we compare making love to a dinner out, there are more trips to McDonald's than to an elegant candle-lit restaurant. The same can be said about receiving communion; most such experiences do not bring spiritual fireworks. Still, Christ is present. Even when husband and wife make love in a cursory fashion, late on a weeknight when both are tired, that experience conveys God's self-gift and their marriage is nourished, body and soul.

At the same time, spouses need to make the effort to have time away by themselves, when lovemaking can happen in the daytime and in leisurely or playful ways. "Good sex, sacramental sex," Andrew Greeley and Mary Greeley Durkin wrote, "needs the same nurturing attention that is given to developing a good prayer life." I would go so far as to say that making love is just as important to a married couple's marital spirituality as participation in the Eucharist is to Christian spirituality in general.

Sadly, even in some cases tragically, down through the decades some Catholic spouses' sexual intimacy and marital spirituality received a crippling blow from widely influential heresies such as Jansenism, which was fueled in no small part by misinterpretations of certain portions of the New Testament. Take Chapter 8 of Paul's Letter to the Romans, for example. Still today, I would wager, many people hear or read Paul's words and misunderstand what he meant to say. Thus:

> For those who live according to the flesh set their minds on the things of the flesh, but those who live according to the Spirit [sometimes translated "spirit"] set their minds on the things of the Spirit [or spirit]. To set the mind on the flesh is death, but to set the mind on the Spirit [or spirit] is life and peace. For this reason the mind that is set on the flesh is hostile to

God; it does not submit to God's law—indeed it cannot, and those who are in the flesh cannot please God.

Countless Christians hear or read these words and, consciously or unconsciously, interpret flesh to mean "sex." But this was not what Paul intended. For Paul, steeped in the culture and traditions of Judaism, there could be no opposition between body and spirit. By "flesh" (Greek, *sarx*), Paul intended primarily social meanings. Anything that would damage the life of the community of faith was a "work of the flesh," an act of the human person alienated from God. Paul included sexual sins on his list, but they were certainly not at the top of his list. Factionalism, jealousy, anger, unfaithfulness, selfishness, these were "works of the flesh" every bit as much as adultery or fornication.

Human sexuality, I am convinced, is one of God's greatest mysteries. For most people, their sexuality can, and often does, mirror God's love in the world. Our sexuality brings us into union with a universe that reflects the goodness of God, both through its power to nourish relationships and the capacity it gives us to procreate. No one who has held a newborn infant is likely to deny that.

A form of spirituality that keys into this cosmic sacramental perspective, and has had an impact on many people in recent decades, is called "creation spirituality" or "creation-centered spirituality." Most closely associated with Matthew Fox, creation spirituality evokes praise from many Catholics and other Christians, while others charge Fox with near-heresy.

The first hurrah for creation spirituality sounded in Matthew Fox's early book, *On Becoming a Musical, Mystical Bear: Whee! We, Wee All the Way Home*, published in 1971 while I was in college. Reading this popular little book, I was struck by Fox's rejection of the traditional ideal of praying for things we need. I wrote the author a letter asking how he could say such a thing when the idea is so clearly present in the

Gospels. Jesus' parable of the persistent widow and the corrupt judge (Luke 18:1–8), for example, clearly encourages praying again and again for what we need. Fox never responded to my letter.

One thing is sure. Since the early 1970s, Matthew Fox's books have been consistent bestsellers, so he is having an impact. When *Original Blessing: A Primer in Creation Spirituality* appeared in 1983, I reviewed it for the *National Catholic Reporter,* and as far as I know it was the only negative review published in any major Catholic periodical. The final line of my review said that reading Fox's book was "not unlike being flogged to death with daffodils." I thought that Fox had a legitimate point, but that his book beat it into the ground; it could have been half as long as it was. Naturally, several Fox fans wrote indignant letters to the editor.

The important question for me was, and is: What is Matthew Fox trying to say? I wondered what other professional theologians might say about his work.

Catholic theologian Rosemary Radford Reuther, who could not be called a conservative, in an article first published in *The Catholic World,* then reprinted a couple of times, including in the *Utne Reader* ("The Best of the Alternative Press"), called Matthew Fox's work "unbalanced." Reuther explained what goes on in Matthew Fox's work.

"Basic to Fox's thought," Reuther wrote, "is that there are two fundamentally opposed types of spirituality in Christianity—a fall-redemption spirituality and a creation-based spirituality."

According to Matthew Fox, fall-redemption spirituality is based on the conviction that human nature and the world around us are fallen, sinful and alienated from God. Fox says that for fall-redemption spirituality salvation comes from above and gives human beings, unworthy as we are, the gift of a redemption that we do not deserve, have no right to ask for, and have no natural capacity to receive.

I had my doubts about this last point; according to Karl Rahner, who by no means would reject fall-redemption spirituality, we have precisely such a capacity, which he called the "supernatural existential." This term simply means that we finite beings have a capacity for union with the infinite love of God.

According to Matthew Fox, we must blame many of the social evils of the twentieth century on fall-redemption spirituality, including the Nazi death camps of World War II, the atomic bomb destruction of Hiroshima and Nagasaki by the United States at the end of the same war, and the torture and execution of thousands upon thousands of Soviet citizens by Joseph Stalin.

In *Original Blessing*, Fox wrote: "The West has been traveling the fall/redemption path for centuries. We all know it; we all have it ingrained in our souls; we have given it 95 percent of our energies in churches both Catholic and Protestant. And look where it has gotten us. Into sexism, militarism, racism, genocide against native peoples, biocide, consumerist capitalism, and violent communism."

I was astonished to discover that Matthew Fox lays virtually the entire blame for all this at the feet of St. Augustine of Hippo, whose *Confessions* I had studied in a college philosophy course taught by a Jesuit professor. Fall-redemption spirituality, Fox said, is rooted in the writings of St. Augustine and received a major shot in the arm from the Protestant Reformation of the sixteenth century.

I squirmed when I read this. I'm no expert on St. Augustine, and I'm not a professional theologian, but I remembered in graduate school reading some of Augustine's commentaries on the creation stories in Genesis, and he said plenty of a positive nature about creation, along with his well-known negative streak when it came to sexuality.

Fall-redemption spirituality, according to Matthew Fox, is dualistic, that is, it divides God from creation, body from soul, and the consciousness of human beings from the natural world. Fox charged fall-redemption spirituality with encouraging people to hate themselves, especially their sexuality.

In *Original Blessing*, Matthew Fox described fall-redemption spirituality as, among other things, "patriarchal" and "ascetic"; it confines itself to one metaphor for God—"Father," and it is "pessimistic."

The more I read Matthew Fox's writing, the more uncomfortable I became. Could a perspective on spirituality that had, admittedly, predominated in the church for so many centuries be so wrong, so bad, the source of so much misery and injustice?

Creation spirituality, the alternative Matthew Fox offers, made some sense to me. Creation spirituality starts with Original Blessing, instead of Original Sin. Borrowing words from Genesis 1:31, it insists that the original and true nature of human beings is "very good." Fox admits that this original and true nature has been distorted by sin and alienation, but it is still our original and authentic self.

Reading as many critiques of Matthew Fox's work as I could locate, and talking with the occasional theologian, I discovered that he is frequently faulted for failing to take sin and evil seriously enough. In response, Fox wrote in *Original Blessing* that sin consists of "injuring creation and doing harm to its balance and harmoniousness, turning what is beautiful into what is ugly."

What about the New Testament's social perspective on sin, I wondered, which views sin as the violation or undermining of interpersonal and communal relationships, our relationships with God and neighbor?

Continuing his discussion of sin, Matthew Fox wrote that "imperfection is integral to all nature." But creation spirituality is "aesthetic." It embraces several metaphors for God, including "Mother" and "Child," as well as "Father." Holiness, according to creation spirituality, is "cosmic hospitality." It encourages "letting go . . . ecstasy, breakthrough."

According to Matthew Fox, salvation should come not as something outside of human nature but as an experience that reunites us with our true nature. Are the two perspectives mutually exclusive? I wondered. Creation spirituality, according to Fox, uncorks liveliness, creativity, and playfulness.

But was it not St. Augustine, I thought, who called the world "a smiling place"?

Reading reviews of Matthew Fox's books, I soon discovered that many of his critics object to how he uses his sources, in Scripture and in the classic writings of the mystics, for example. He seems capable of finding support for creation spirituality just about anyplace. He overlooks sentences and paragraphs that reflect fall-redemption spirituality and gloms onto those he can interpret to mirror creation spirituality.

Trying to distill everything I had read and heard about creation spirituality, I came to the conclusion that it is unfair to build up an opposition between fall-redemption spirituality and creation spirituality. We need them both. Both are present in the Bible and in sacred tradition. Yes, the universe is a sacrament or, in David Tracy's terms, an analogy for God. We need to love, honor, and respect ourselves and all of creation. Yes, we need to remember that for St. Paul, anyone who is "in Christ" is "a new creation." But, to borrow images from Genesis, we can't live as if Adam and Eve never sinned, we can't live as if they were never banished from Paradise.

I believe that we need to take Original Sin seriously, just as we must take Original Blessing seriously. Those who reject fall-redemption spirituality are just as unbalanced as those who reject creation spirituality. Both are necessary to a mature spirituality; each acts as a corrective and balance to the other.

Eight

God Loves Everyone the Same

One of the most obvious things about being a Catholic school kid is uniforms. They vary from school to school, but Catholic school uniforms are hard to mistake. Uniforms are such a good idea that today some government schools put kids in uniforms, too.

I get the impression that some, perhaps many, Catholic high schools no longer require uniforms. If I may be permitted a contrary opinion, I think that's a mistake. In an era when individualism is bloated all out of proportion, I think uniforms for Catholic high school students would make a statement about the need sometimes for individual identity to give way to one's membership in a community. School uniforms could also reflect the need to ignore the dictates of the fashion industry, now and then. This is a lesson Catholic high school students could benefit from when they are the objects—I almost said victims—of billion-dollar-a-year marketing campaigns.

Sure, we complained, we moaned, we gave our parents endless grief about having to wear uniforms to school. But we also learned a lesson, and it goes like this: What's on the outside is incidental; what's in the heart is what matters, because God loves everyone the same.

When I began attending a Catholic school in my third grade year, before long I made friends with a boy my own age who had a cleft palate—or to use the more common and more cruel term, a "harelip." Larry was on the roly-poly side, as well, and he was the best and most faithful friend a kid could want.

One day I informed our teacher, Sister Angelica, that "me 'n' Larry" were going to do something or other. "Mean Larry?" she responded. "Is Larry mean?" Thus was "S'ter" always on the lookout for errant grammar. *"Larry and I,"* I corrected myself.

Larry's cleft palate had been surgically repaired to the extent medical science could manage in the late 1940s, and he had the distinctive scar on his upper lip. Remarkably, Larry's birth defect mattered not at all. I don't remember him ever being teased about it, and it never came up in our conversation. His cleft palate was irrelevant. For we spent our days in a Catholic school environment that constantly cultivated caring for others for what they were, not for how they looked.

This is a lesson I took to heart, and many times in later life I found myself able to look past or through externals to the heart of the person, regardless of physical features, race, or manner of dress. Even today, this experience helps when I encounter a teenage boy who wears several earrings in one ear, or with his hair clipped in a style I find alarming. (It's getting more and more difficult to disturb adults, is it not?) Largely because of what I learned in Catholic schools, I believe that a drunk on the street is equal in humanity to the president of the United States.

In essence, what I learned in Catholic school was the importance of the virtue of justice. But I learned it mostly through daily experience, not from a book. The *Baltimore Catechism* didn't exactly fall all over itself teaching about social justice. Its treatment of the subject was cursory, at best. The answer to Question 132 explained that the "chief moral virtues" or "cardinal virtues" are: prudence, justice, fortitude, and temperance.

"How do prudence, justice, fortitude, and temperance dispose us to lead good lives?" asked Question 134, and the answer with regard to justice said: "Justice disposes us to give everyone what belongs to him." The commentary went into more detail: "Justice perfects the will and safeguards the chief rights of man; his right to life and freedom, to the sanctity of the home, to his good name and honor, and to his external possessions."

All this was good as far as it went, but I don't recall a whale of a lot of emphasis on the implications of these ideas. When we talked about sin, for example, Sister Angelica didn't say boo about sins against justice.

Peace got even less attention. In its answer to Question 129, the old catechism quoted the seventh beatitude from the Sermon on the Mount: "Blessed are the peacemakers, for they shall be called children of God." We memorized the Beatitudes, and that was the end of that.

Pope Leo XIII, in the late nineteenth century wrote encyclicals with a powerful social message, but his thoughts didn't make it into the *Baltimore Catechism*. It would take the Second Vatican Council and *Pacem in Terris*, the great encyclical on peace by Pope John XXIII, to make "justice and peace" a topic of widespread Catholic interest.

Still, the spirit of justice and the spirit of peace were alive in the Catholic schools I attended, even if we rarely talked about them. I believe the old catechism and our everyday Catholic school experience sowed seeds in the hearts of many young Catholics that would bear fruit in the years following the Second Vatican Council.

Even prior to the Council, there were Catholic prophets of justice at large in the land, people who studied documents such as *Rerum Novarum*, a landmark encyclical by Pope Leo XIII, and tried to act on them. They were deeply influenced by this encyclical, in which the pope spoke out against the inhuman conditions working people had to tolerate in industrial societies, and by his call for economic justice.

During the 1930s, '40s and '50s, Catholics such as Dorothy Day and John LaFarge, S.J., laid the groundwork for the day when the American bishops would issue pastoral letters on topics such as war and peace, and the American economy, as they did in the 1980s.

Dorothy Day's story is well known, and there is no need for me to tell it again. As co-founder with Peter Maurin of the Catholic Worker movement, she accomplished a heroic blend of personal spirituality and dedication to working for social justice. By her life and actions, Dorothy Day called the world and the church to a concern for social justice during years when countless Catholic school kids, like me, hadn't a clue as to the church's teachings on social justice.

I have heard that a few Catholic high schools in the east and midwest had faculty members who knew what was what in the church when it came to social justice. I have heard stories of Catholic high school and university students who were involved with the Catholic Worker movement in the decades I'm talking about. But in the Pacific Northwest, I don't think this was ever so. In this case, we probably fit the conviction held by Catholics in other parts of the country that everything west of the continental divide was small potatoes.

Father John LaFarge is another example. An American Jesuit priest from a privileged social background, he used the power of the pen to proclaim messages of peace and justice, for many years on the staff of the Jesuit weekly magazine, *America*. During an era when American Catholics were fascinated to no end by the promises of the Blessed Virgin at Fatima, and when nuns lectured adolescent female students on the virtues of wearing "Mary-like" dresses, Father LaFarge urged Catholics to take the social teachings of the church more seriously. He wanted Catholics to get involved in the wider society for the sake of Christ's kingdom of peace and justice. He had a deep concern for the poor, and as early as the 1930s he wrote books on the evils of racism.

In other words, during the years when I attended Catholic elementary and secondary schools there was some significant Catholic concern for peace and justice issues, even at the highest levels of the church, but this rarely filtered into the wider

Catholic community and into the Catholic schools, not the ones
I attended, at least. I never heard about *Rerum Novarum*, and
I never heard about Dorothy Day and Father John LaFarge
until years later. When I was in the fourth grade, it was a big
deal to see a film about Father Patrick Peyton and his Rosary
Crusade.

My sensitivity to social justice concerns lay dormant, or
were nonexistent, through four years in the U.S. Navy. I saw no
reason to object to the war in Vietnam. The official line
sounded reasonable to me, that American military personnel
were there to save the world from communism. Safely en-
sconced on a U.S. Marine Corps air station in Hawaii, I watched
hundreds of young marines pass through on their way to com-
bat assignments in Vietnam and thanked my lucky stars I
wasn't going with them. I pitied the Navy medical corpsmen
who were assigned to marine corps units.

During 1968, when the anti-war movement heated up, I
watched, mystified, as the TV network news programs ran
footage of militant students taking over university campuses,
and the national guard killings at Kent State. When President
Lyndon Johnson appeared in public, anti-war protestors interrupted him with their chant: "LBJ! LBJ! How many kids have
you killed today?"

I was excited when Bobby Kennedy declared his candidacy
for president, and I felt physically sick one morning in June
when an empty-headed young sailor informed me in a flippant
tone of voice that Kennedy had been killed while walking
through the kitchen of a hotel in Los Angeles.

During my sophomore year in college, I read a book that,
for the first time, opened my mind to the vital importance of
peace and justice issues in any Christian life. It was *No Bars to
Manhood*, by Daniel Berrigan, S.J. A friend was majoring in
political science, and I had never been able to understand why;
it sounded like such a boring major. After reading Berrigan's
book, I told him I could see why he would be interested in
political science. "Politics is *everything*," I said enthusiastically.

It wasn't long before I read Henry David Thoreau's *Civil Disobedience* and learned that there was a strain of political nonconformity for the sake of social justice even in the literature of nineteenth-century secular America.

Years before, I had read Thomas Merton's early books, his autobiography, *The Seven Storey Mountain, The Sign of Jonas,* and *No Man Is an Island.* Now I read what he had written about peace and justice issues, including war and racism. I read *Seeds of Destruction* and *Faith and Violence,* and I began to discover the intimate connections between prayer, spirituality and the peace and justice issues that were so prominent during the 1960s and early '70s.

As with developments in my spirituality during my college years, my biblical studies opened doors for me with regard to social justice, too. I learned that the concept of social justice is one of the most basic themes in the Bible. Speaking through the prophet Amos, for example, the Lord declares that justice is more important than pious celebrations and gatherings: "I hate, I despise your festivals, and I take no delight in your solemn assemblies. . . . Take away from me the noise of your songs; I will not listen to the melody of your harps. But let justice roll down like waters, and righteousness like an everflowing stream" (5:21–24).

In Luke's Gospel, when Jesus begins his public ministry, he applies to himself words that echo the prophet Isaiah's call for social justice, healing and peace: "The Spirit of the Lord is upon me, because he has anointed me to bring good news to the poor. He has sent me to proclaim release to the captives, and recovery of sight to the blind, to let the oppressed go free. . . . " (4:18).

Studying the Gospel of Matthew, I began to see that the beatitudes have a profoundly social meaning. The beatitude "Blessed are the peacemakers . . . " (5:9) that I had memorized from the old catechism years before had meanings I could not have imagined at the time, and those meanings couldn't help but be social and political in nature.

While in college, I first read the earth-shaking 1963 encyclical of Pope John XXIII, *Pacem in Terris*. Peace, Pope John wrote, must be based on a social order "founded on truth, built according to justice, vivified and integrated by charity, and put into practice in freedom."

I was touched by Pope John's call for all committed Christians to work together to build local, national, and world institutions which would respect the dignity of human beings and encourage justice and peace. He even called for a world government that would respect and protect the rights of all people. Human beings have social and economic rights, Pope John wrote, not just political and legal rights.

Some conservative Catholics disliked, and, I suppose, still dislike, this kind of talk, especially coming from a pope. In the course of my graduate studies in theology at Marquette, I studied the writings of the great nineteenth-century English convert to Catholicism, Cardinal John Henry Newman. One of my favorite Newman quotations is from his famous book, *An Essay On the Development of Christian Doctrine:* "Nay, one cause of corruption in religion is the refusal to follow the course of doctrine as it moves on, and an obstinacy in the notions of the past."

On Sunday morning in the autumn of 1972, I watched a family walk out in the middle of a homily in a California parish church. A man stood up, shouted, "Priests shouldn't talk about politics!" and then he and his wife and three or four young children left. If anyone had been dozing through the homily, they woke up after that!

The priest had been preaching on the reading from Luke's Gospel quoted above, and he had related it to a statement from the *Pastoral Constitution on the Church in the Modern World*. I know the exact sentence, because later that day I underlined it in my copy of the Vatican II documents: "Excessive economic and social disparity between individuals and peoples of the one human race is a source of scandal and militates against social justice, equity, human dignity, as well as social and international peace" (art. 29).

Another book I read while in college gave me further insights into what was going on in the world, insights that remain valid to this day. That book was Barbara Ward's 1963 classic, *The Rich Nations and the Poor Nations*.

Barbara Ward wrote that

> our world today is dominated by a complex and tragic division. One part of mankind has undergone the revolutions of modernization and has emerged on the other side to a pattern of great and increasing wealth. But most of the rest of mankind has yet to achieve any of the revolutions; they are caught off balance before the great movement of economic and social momentum can be launched. Their old traditional world is dying. The new radical world is not yet born. This being so, the gap between the rich and the poor has become inevitably the most tragic and urgent problem of our day.

Later, while in graduate school at Marquette, I met a young Jesuit priest from India named Ignatius Jesudasan, who was working on a doctorate in theology. As I recall, his dissertation had something to do, appropriately enough, with Gandhi. At any rate, I was struck by this Indian Jesuit, particularly his simplicity. He came from a poor country, and here he was plunked down in the United States, surrounded by what must have seemed incredible wealth, and he took it all in stride. His Jesuit provincial sent him to this country to earn a doctorate in theology, and he stayed here until he did that. There were no visits home in the summertime, his province couldn't afford it. He lived simply, dressed simply, worked hard, and was a quiet, thoughtful, smiling man with no pretentions about anything.

From watching and listening to Ignatius Jesudasan I began to see that ultimately the differences between the rich and the poor come down to lifestyle choices. As a society, and as individuals, we make choices about how we are going to live, and those choices affect not just us but, ultimately, the entire world.

If one country, the United States for example, consumes more than its share of the world's resources, that choice means that countless millions of people do not get their fair share. There is enough for all, but not enough for all to make pigs of themselves. It's as simple as that.

I began to see that the affluence the average American craves carries with it a poverty of its own, a poverty of spirit with tragic dimensions. From this perspective, "more is less."

Sometime along the way, I read *The Pursuit of Loneliness*, by sociologist Phillip Slater. His analysis of the connections between our insatiable craving for possessions and our emotional emptiness remains, I believe, a valid critique of the American way of life consistent with thoughts that appear in the writings of Pope John Paul II.

Teaching college freshmen at a Catholic university in the early 1980s, I assigned Slater's book as a text and was amazed at how deeply many students resented its message. The Reagan years were upon us, and I couldn't believe how reluctant my students were to ask questions or criticize anything about the dominant American culture. As far as they were concerned, there was a fat apple pie waiting for them out there, and they were anxious to cut themselves a big piece of it. Period.

A few years later, I read Jesuit Father John Francis Cavanaugh's *Following Christ in a Consumer Society: The Spirituality of Cultural Resistance*. This book helped me to better understand the tension that exists between the spirit of the gospel and the dominant American culture. I was especially impressed by one passage in Cavanaugh's book:

> Let us suppose you are a married person with children. If you are relatively happy with your life, if you enjoy spending time with your children, playing with them and talking with them; if you like nature, if you enjoy sitting in your yard or on your front steps, if your sexual life is relatively happy, if you have a peaceful sense of who you are and are stabilized in your relationships, if you like to pray in solitude, if

you just like talking to people, visiting them, spending
time in conversation with them, if you enjoy living
simply, if you sense no need to compete with your
friends or neighbors—*what good are you economi-
cally* in terms of our system? You haven't spent a
nickle yet.

What can it mean, I wondered, to live in a society where
most people believe that money is the ultimate reality? In his
novel *Needful Things,* one of Stephen King's characters asks,
"Why do so many people think that all the answers are in their
wallet?" What can it mean to live in a society where people believe that even personal commitments like marriage and
parenthood depend absolutely on the ability to maintain affluence? Is it possible to live in the United States and take the
Sermon on the Mount seriously?

Following graduate school, in 1976, my wife, Kathy, and I
accepted a shared position directing religious education programs in a parish in Bremerton, Washington, across Puget
Sound from Seattle. This led to our first close encounter with
the "military-industrial complex" we had heard so much
about. The nearby shipyard was the construction site for Trident nuclear submarines, sea-going war machines of gargantuan proportions designed to carry nuclear warheads with a
destructive potential far beyond what leveled Hiroshima and
Nagasaki in August, 1945.

Near the Trident base, Jim and Shelley Douglas directed
Ground Zero, a center for anti-nuclear education and protest.
We never visited Ground Zero, but we read the little newspaper
it published, and we were impressed when the Archbishop of
Seattle, Raymond Hunthausen, participated in protest actions
sponsored by Ground Zero.

Since the parish we worked in was so near the Trident base,
naturally many members of the parish worked in one aspect or
another of the "defense" industry. We found this disturbing.
Clearly, it seemed to us, building nuclear weapons and the
machines to launch them was contrary to modern church

teachings. Our own archbishop had announced that he would refuse to pay the percentage of his federal taxes that would go to the national defense budget. Yet these people and, by extension, the parish itself depended on the business of building Trident submarines for financial well-being.

In the spring of 1977, Kathy and I decided that we were obliged to "do something." So we did something stupid. I wrote a letter to Archbishop Hunthausen in which I expressed our frustration at working in a parish on the doorstep of the Trident base, yet never had the pastor said one thing about this issue; never had he tried to bring it up for discussion or dialogue within the parish. This implied that the pastor didn't want to upset or alienate his parishioners by suggesting that they earned their livelihood in immoral ways.

Without bringing our concern to the pastor first (dumb, dumb), which was unfair to him, Kathy and I signed the letter and mailed it to Archbishop Hunthausen, and I dropped off a copy at the pastor's office. In the meantime, we had accepted another position in another diocese, so, of course, we were taking no risk at all by writing this letter. Like I said: stupid. Probably cowardly, as well.

The pastor was upset because our letter would make him look bad to the archbishop. He gave us copies of sermons he had preached against the war in Vietnam. He wrote a letter to the bishop in the diocese we were moving to, informing him of what we had done, then he kept the letter for a few days, keeping us in suspense. One Saturday morning he slipped his letter under our front door, without knocking, to show that he had decided not to mail it. Lucky for us.

All in all, it was a pathetic event from beginning to end, our little foray into standing up for peace and justice.

Trying to relate our life as a family to international issues like nuclear arms was one thing. Another is our ongoing attempt to relate our everyday values and lifestyle to global realities. We joined an organization in our diocese called Adopt-a-Family, which matches families in our diocese and a few other parts of the country with Quiché Indian families who live in the mountains of Guatemala. We were first matched with a young married couple, Marcelo and Avila, and their children, and each month we sent Adopt-a-Family $30 to help "our" family to become self-sufficient.

A couple of years later, in 1989, we visited Guatemala for a few days and met Marcelo, Avila, and their children. This was one of the most moving experiences of our lives and it has had a continuing influence on our determination to live our family life from a faith-informed social justice perspective.

Fields of rustling, bright green cornstalks lined both sides of the rutted dirt road. The cornstalks were fifteen feet high if they were an inch. Men, women, and children, dressed in the traditional bright colors of Guatemala's highlands, moved to the sides of the road as our red Toyota Land Rover growled along in second gear. The late afternoon sun was golden in the deep blue sky. Huge gray clouds began to gather for the heavy rain that would fall that night.

Our driver and guide, Sister Marie Tolle, a missionary for our diocese, called out over the complaints of the rocking, lurching vehicle's engine that we were almost there. "Here we are!" Sister Marie drove the Land Rover as far off the road as possible, so that when she opened her door she had to push back corn stalks in order to climb out.

Away from the road some dozen yards stood the new home of Marcelo and Avila, thick adobe brick walls halfway up, then horizontal boards. Guatemalans call the roofing material *lamina*. It's the waved, corrugated tin roofing often used in the United States on sheds and utility buildings.

Marcelo and Avila, their faces beaming with broad smiles, came out to meet us. Both are short of stature by American standards. Marcelo is slender with sharp features, Avila is a beautiful young Quiché woman with long, shining black hair. Everyone embraced, and for the moment there seemed to be no need for a common language.

"They've been looking forward to this ever since I told them you were coming two months ago," Sister Marie said. "They are so excited they hardly know what to do with themselves." The children smiled and clung to their parents—a five-year-old girl, a boy, three, and a one-year-old girl whose birthday was that very day.

Marcelo beckoned everyone into the house, and Avila brought small, unpainted wooden chairs for each person. The main room of their house, about twenty-five by fifteen feet, contained two double beds and one single bed, a small table against one wall, and a chest of drawers painted white. Photographs of friends and relatives decorated the walls. A simple crucifix hung in a place of honor, and a bare light bulb hung from the rafters in the middle of the room. For the occasion, the cement floor was spread with fresh, sweet-smelling pine needles.

Through a wide doorway to the right as we entered was the kitchen and dining area. Marcelo and Avila have a brick stove and chimney, and their home is a marvel in a part of the world where most people still cook over a smokey open fire in a thatched-roof hut with walls made of dried cornstalks lashed together.

Marcelo invited everyone to be seated. Then with some formality he handed Sister Marie a statement he had written and asked her to translate it from Spanish into English for everyone to hear.

"Dear Brother and Sister from the U.S.," the letter began.

"Good afternoon. We rejoice that you visit us this afternoon, and welcome you to our humble home."

Marcelo's statement gave "a short history of our home," beginning with his and Avila's wedding day, March 8, 1981. Marcelo recounted the births of their three children and told of the years during which he spent all of his weekdays working in distant Guatemala City. After three years he had earned enough money to buy *lamina* for the house he wanted to build for his family. Still, he didn't have enough money to buy the other materials and pay for construction. "I began to look for a loan but I didn't receive one."

Marcelo heard that a family in the United States might help him through a program called *Familia a Familia,* which Sister

Marie was connected with. "Then in the first months of 1985, with your help we were able to build our house. . . . I obtained potable water in our house, and electric light, and by the year '86 I no longer had to go to work in the capital and began to live with my family in the house . . . . So with your help, we lived during this time, using the money for food and clothing for our children."

Marcelo's statement concluded: "Brother and Sister, we do not have any way to thank you for the favor you have done us. You have helped us in our great need. Thank you and may God repay you. All you have done for us you have done for God."

As Sister Marie read, Kathy and I had tears in our eyes, and by the time she finished we had a difficult time trying to think what to say. We had descended on these good people, and their gratitude for the bit of help we had given them was boundless, yet they expressed it with great dignity and pride.

I felt ashamed of myself for the many months that I wrote out $30 checks that would go to this family as if I were doing nothing more than paying another bill. But I also felt deeply touched by Marcelo's strength and his love for his wife and children. Sister Marie translated my stumbling words: "Marcelo and Avila, you have a beautiful family and a beautiful home, and you are a great blessing to us."

Kathy gave Avila a snapshot of our family in a cloth frame she made and decorated with a colorful needlepoint design. Our three boys, then ages nine, seven, and six, grinned from the photo like wiseacres. Marcelo said that he and Avila had wanted such a picture more than anything, so they could see what their American friends look like and remember them.

With a little encouragement, Marcelo picked up a battered guitar with one string missing and played a lively tune. Everyone applauded, then Avila invited us into the kitchen and dining area.

We put our chairs around a well-used rough wood table, a smaller version of the average American picnic table. The table was covered with a thin plastic Christmas tablecloth decorated around the edges with *Feliz Navidad!*

The baby giggled in a plain wood high chair Marcelo had built, and Avila served glasses of a thin hot chocolate beverage—an extravagance in our honor. Marcelo passed around a plate of sweetened white rolls.

After our snack, everyone moved outside to take pictures. We stood together and smiled for the camera. Two days later, after a stopover in Mexico City, we were back in our own home with its two stories, five bedrooms, big living room and dining room, wall-to-wall carpeting, large kitchen, and wraparound porch with a porch swing that faces a tree-filled park across the street.

Our few days in Guatemala taught me more about peace and justice than any other experience I have ever had. It taught me that "peace and justice" is an abstraction. What we're talking about, when we talk about "peace and justice" is people, real human beings like Marcelo and Avila and their children.

Over the years, as Kathy and I became parents and began to struggle with raising a family of our own, the connections between justice and peace and family life have become more and more evident to us. I believe that what is good for a family is what will be good for the church, for the nation, and, ultimately, for the world. Now, whenever an issue of a social, cultural or economic nature arises, the first question I ask myself is: What will the impact be on our family and families in general?

I admire the Amish a good deal for the ways they respond to modern society, yet I do not find myself inclined to distance myself from "the world" as they do. One of the main things I admire about the Amish is their determination to evaluate almost everything in terms of its impact on family and community life.

Donald B. Craybill, in his little book, *The Puzzles of Amish Life,* explained the outlook on life and the world cultivated by the Amish. Craybill wrote:

Without the aid of consultants or the benefits of higher
education, [the Amish] have created a different world,
a world without welfare recipients, homeless vaga-
bonds and illegitimate children. A world where stress
workshops are unknown and where drug and alcohol
abuse are almost nil. A world where divorce is
unknown, truancy is unheard-of and violent crime is
rare. . . . By negotiating with modern life, the Amish
have bypassed the pitfalls of progress while tapping
enough of its resources to maintain a viable community. In all these ways the Amish press us to explore
the meaning of progress and ponder what it means to
be 'ahead' or 'behind.'

Many people think it merely strange that the Amish refuse
to own cars, radios, television sets, and many of the other technological wonders of the modern era. You will find no stereo
system in an Amish home and no telephone. The Amish
believe that these things will erode the quality of family and
community life, and who can argue with them? The next time a
teenager spends hours talking on the telephone, think about the
Amish. If they were to buy cars, the Amish believe, soon family
members would be running in all directions at all hours, and
their teenagers would be getting themselves into trouble.

The rest of the world welcomes with open arms every new
technological development and asks questions later, if at all. If
family relationships suffer as one result of television's presence
in the home, it's the family's fault, not television's. If
teenagers are rarely home and so become strangers to their
parents, the automobile has nothing to do with it. Few question
the value of microwave ovens and automatic garage door
openers.

If they had radios and television, the Amish would un-
avoidably expose themselves to a value system that cares
nothing for their faith in God, is hedonistic and aghast at their
dedication to a simple way of life. If the Amish had stereo
music systems in their homes, where would the quiet go, and

what would happen to all the opportunities they have to talk with one another? What would happen to the quiet times when they can simply listen to their own hearts where, perchance, God may speak?

The ultimate value for the Amish is simplicity for the sake of right relationships with God and neighbor. We may not wish to live like the Amish, but a question hovers in the air. What kind of place would the world be if more people lived more like the Amish do?

I admire the Amish concern to maintain the integrity and health of family and community life. But our family follows their example in only one major respect. Since before our children were born, we have not owned a television set. Mr. Rogers did not cultivate the self-esteem of our three sons during their preschool years. They did not learn the alphabet from "Sesame Street," and their little psyches were not pummeled by hundreds upon hundreds of commercials for breakfast cereals and candy on Saturday mornings, interrupted now and then by cartoon programs of questionable value, even as entertainment.

We chose to have a television-free home because this was one way we could regain a significant degree of control over our environment. To welcome television into our home, we believe, would be to invite into the heart of our family life a value system that in some basic ways is incompatible with the Gospel of Jesus and with a Catholic-Christian spirituality and lifestyle for our time.

By the simple act of giving TV the heave-ho, we made room for more opportunities to interact with one another, often peacefully, but sometimes not. Regardless, we relate to one another; we can't escape by zoning out on television. We read. Sometimes we play games. We simply hang out. If a kid wants to talk to a parent, or a parent wants to talk to a kid, it's difficult to do that with a television images competing for everyone's attention.

People sometimes ask why not have a TV set and regulate it strictly. We could have done that, and we know people who do.

Our rationale is simple: We took the easy way out. Doing without television entirely is easier than trying to regulate it, and no
TV at all makes it easier to cultivate a Christian counter-cultural
spirit in our home.

Life without television is a good life, but it is an experiment. We won't know the lasting effects on our children, if
any, until they are adults. At minimum, we doubt that we are
doing them any harm. At maximum, a television-free home
may help all the members of our family to think more clearly
and to read more; it may enable our children to make better
choices later in life because maybe their noggins will be less
cluttered with some of the sillier forms of cultural detritus than
the noggins of their peers.

Nine

Nobody's Perfect

I was driving along one hot September afternoon, and at a red light I eased to a stop behind another car. I noticed a sticker with bright red letters on the bumper in front of me and peered over my steering wheel to see what it said. "I SURVIVED CATHOLIC SCHOOL" the sticker announced.

This is not the kind of public relations Catholic schools need, I thought. On the other hand, it is true that some people who attended Catholic schools do not look back on those years fondly. Some are even bitter and angry. Some people tell stories about Catholic school nuns that make the witch in *The Wizard of Oz* look like Rebecca of Sunnybrook Farm.

Even today I can identify. Sister A., principal of the Catholic school our three sons attended, called one morning to report that there had been "an incident" with one of our sons. He and his teacher, an older nun, had locked horns. Our son wanted to do things one way, Sister wanted him to do them another way. Push came to shove, and she locked our son out of the classroom, an action we objected to, regardless of what he did or did not do.

We consulted with a school psychologist friend and concluded that our son and this particular Catholic school were not a good match. Well-meaning though she was, the principal's rigid educational philosophy would brook no adaptations; it was tow the line or get out, end of discussion.

We were painfully disappointed by this, even though we found a government school alternative education program where our son was as happy as a clam at high tide. There he found a loosely structured, stimulating school environment where each student was allowed to progress at his or her own pace. Still, we felt betrayed by a Catholic school. If a government school program could provide a comfortable learning environment for our son, why couldn't a Catholic school do at least as much?

Then I remembered that all had not been sweetness and light when I was our son's age. I remembered times when Sister Angelica lost her temper and threw a chalkboard eraser at a kid in the back of the room. When I was a third grader, Sister forced me to stand at the chalkboard in tears until I could finish a problem in long division.

Some months before my parents decided that we would become Catholics, for no apparent reason Sister Angelica verbally browbeat me in the presence of the entire class for not being a Catholic; I might not think the Catholic Church was "the one true church," but I was wrong. Talk about mortified. I was eight years old, for crying out loud, and I didn't have the faintest idea what she was talking about.

Yesterday's Catholic schools were not perfect, and neither are today's. Because their financial resources are severely limited, sometimes Catholic schools are not able to provide the kinds of services a gifted child needs, and the same goes for a child with a learning disability. Sometimes Catholic elementary schools, especially, are best suited to children who are more or less average; if a child has some special need, parents may find it necessary to send that child elsewhere in order to meet that need.

I don't mean to imply that in all situations a government school will be able to "take up the slack." In some parts of the country, government schools are even less capable of helping gifted or learning disabled children. All a parent can do is investigate the options and make the best choice possible.

In the long run, what I learned from attending less-than-perfect Catholic schools was that this is the way the world is. It's unfair to expect perfection in either people or institutions. This may sound obvious, but there are people who never get over the discovery that perfection is not available even where they most hoped to discover it.

If you scratch just beneath the surface of the cynics who slap "I SURVIVED CATHOLIC SCHOOL" bumper stickers on their cars, I suspect that you'll find disillusioned idealists, people who are bitterly disappointed to have found flawed people teaching in a school that failed to meet their expectations. They are not about to forgive those who showed them that the world is less than a perfect place, even in a Catholic school.

The same people may reject the Catholic Church, too, and for similar reasons. The church is filled with some great saints, some great sinners, and the rest of us who fall someplace along a wide spectrum between the two extremes.

Chances are, people who bad-mouth Catholic schools have a legitimate reason for doing so. Tom, a former Catholic high school honor student, drifted away from the church in the late 1960s, after graduating from a Catholic university. He complains about being "emotionally abused" by nuns when he was in grade school. "They damaged my self-esteem in ways that I still struggle with today," he said.

Martha attended Catholic elementary and secondary schools and wants nothing to do with the church. She calls herself "a recovering Catholic" and blames her past drug abuse and current emotional and weight-control problems on "all the guilt the nuns laid on me." Martha reads one pop psychology self-help author after another, searching endlessly for some way to get her life together.

The charges Tom and Martha level at the Catholic schools they attended may be justified to one degree or another. It is also possible that they seized on Catholic schools as a place to lay the blame for difficulties they would have encountered regardless of what kind of schools they attended.

Martin A. Lang, author of *Acquiring Our Image of God: The Emotional Basis for Religious Education*, says that there is a close connection between one's relationship with the church and a person's relationship with his or her parents. People whose bond with their parents was not strong early in life may not bond well with their parents' faith community, either. "Weak bonding [with parents]," Lang says, "for whatever reasons, is a hindrance to deep religious affiliation and religious experience."

Consistent with Martin A. Lang's line of thought, an adult's rejection of the church today may have little to do with anything about the church itself. Such a rejection may be, more than anything else, an extended adolescent rebellion against one's parents and the things associated with them. There are, of course, exceptions to every theory. It is perfectly possible that one who bonded weakly with his or her parents might turn to the church as a kind of surrogate family.

In hindsight, it may seem that particular Catholic schools of the 1930s, '40s and '50s were not entirely healthy places. On the other hand, I suspect that you'll find far more people, like me, who had predominantly good experiences in pre–Vatican II Catholic schools. The same goes for the Catholic schools of today. Each should be evaluated on its own merits, on an individual basis. Some are better than others, and there are probably a few genuinely bad ones. Still, it's grossly unfair to condemn all Catholic schools on the basis of finding a few bad ones, either yesterday or today. Again, this may sound obvious, but some people do precisely this.

I met an old friend who attended the same Catholic high school as I, but he had stopped practicing the Catholic faith years ago. He went on at some length about how "messed up" his life was. He had been involved in a "relationship" with a woman who had two children from a failed marriage. Even though they had not married, he trusted her enough to buy a house with her. Soon thereafter, she announced that she didn't love him anymore. Still, he was responsible for the payments on the house the two of them bought together, plus the payments on the house he had purchased prior to meeting her.

My friend from years gone by complained that all his money was going to pay lawyers who were trying to free him from his obligation to make payments on the second house. If leaving the church is such a good idea, I wondered, why is he so miserable?

If my friend had not abandoned the Catholic faith, along with a more or less traditional Catholic code of personal ethics, his life would not be so "messed up." He would not have chosen to live with a woman to whom he was not married; indeed, he might never have met her because he would have drawn his friends from a Christian faith community. The point is not that "practicing one's faith" guarantees against mistakes and unhappiness, but the chances of veering so far off course are greatly reduced.

People leave the church, perhaps, because they believe that outside the church they will find more freedom. Instead, they frequently find less freedom and more unhappiness.

Another friend from high school days attended the reunion to celebrate the twentieth anniversary of our graduation. One of the brightest students in our class, his life had been on a downhill slide for years. In the late 1960s, while in college, he "got a girl pregnant," married her, never finished college, and had some seventeen years of marital misery. Chain-smoking unfiltered cigarettes, he told me that he was recently divorced, and his two daughters were causing him constant anxiety. He was yet another example of an old friend whose life crashed. Again, I would say that the most basic reason this happened was that he chose to abandon the church and a Catholic-Christian code of personal morality.

My old friends are both examples of people who leave the church because they "see no purpose in it," or some other equally vague rationale. The church isn't perfect, it doesn't measure up to their expectations, it seems "outmoded," or a priest or nun did or said something they found offensive, so they leave the church. This implies that living a life guided by "what's happening now" is a superior way to go. Which brings me back to my previous question: If abandoning the Catholic faith is such a good idea, why are my ex-Catholic friends so unhappy?

There are probably ex-Catholics who now practice no religion whose lives are on a more-or-less even keel, who are not depressed and plagued by anxious questions about the meaning of it all. Still, I believe that the chances of having a healthy, meaningful life are greater inside than outside a Christian faith community. Another religious tradition may be an option, but to turn to the dominant culture and follow its trends and fashions as the way to live one's life is to ask for serious trouble.

The church isn't perfect. Far from it. When I was working on a book about ten key moments in church history (*Time Capsules of the Church*), I was impressed by how during the sixteenth century the Catholic Church might have been able to avoid the final split that took place between Catholicism and the Reformation. The Council of Trent (1545–1563) must accept some of the blame for that.

While doing research for the chapter in my book on the First Vatican Council (1869–1870), I was surprised to learn that the pope responsible for the doctrine on papal infallibility, Pius IX, was most likely senile at the time of the Council. I quoted Catholic journalist Peter Hebblethwaite's outstanding biography, *Pope John XXIII: Shepherd of the Modern World*: "The truth is that Pius IX, who was seventy-eight when the council began, was often an embarrassment and was regarded by some of the Fathers of Vatican I as gaga."

The history of the church is rife with examples of corruption and immorality at all levels. There are scandals in every other chapter. Even today, church leaders sometimes speak and act as if Christ did not come to set us free but to offer us a new set of chains. While I was in college, I first read the classic literary critique of church leaders, a story in Fyodor Dostoyevsky's *The Brothers Karamazov* called "The Grand Inquisitor."

In the story, Jesus has returned to earth. He raises a little girl, lying in her coffin, back to life. A tall, dark, brooding

Cardinal Inquisitor, ninety years old, witnesses the miracle and has Jesus arrested. Visiting Jesus in his prison cell, the Inquisitor tells him that he should not have "interfered." Before he died on the cross, Jesus gave his authority to the leaders of the church, and now they have everything under control. Because he has come back and is interfering, tomorrow morning Jesus will be burned at the stake, and at one word from the Inquisitor the people will help to heap the burning coals at his feet.

The brooding Cardinal Inquisitor acknowledges that when Jesus came the first time he came to set people free. But people can't cope with being free, he says, so church leaders make people think they are free by telling them in Jesus' name what to think and do.

Dostoyevsky's story bears much meditation on the part of all Catholics. There is always the temptation for church leaders to abuse their authority like the Grand Inquisitor does, and there is always the temptation for believers to take refuge in the false security of blind obedience.

Catholicism has a shadow side, according to Franciscan Father Richard Rohr and theologian Joseph Martos, in their book, *Why Be Catholic?* "A good person radiates light into the lives of those around. Great and influential people are bright lights in history: They do much good, but they also can do much harm. The same is true of great institutions, such as the Catholic Church."

We couldn't get along without the institutional church, Rohr and Martos say, from parish and diocesan institutions to national church institutions and those of the Vatican. The institutional church does much good. But the institutional church also has a dark side. We see this when people identify the church, as a whole, with its institutions or with the clergy and hierarchy. We see this dark side when Catholics in general don't think of themselves as the church. We see this when Catholics don't hear the words of Christ addressed to them but only to priests and religious. We see this dark side when Catholics don't take responsibility for the church's mission in the world but pass the buck, instead, to church institutions.

The great German Catholic theologian of the 1940s and '50s, Monsignor Romano Guardini, referred to the church's shadow side when he said that the church is the cross Christ was crucified on.

Father Andrew Greeley, the noted author and sociologist and probably the single most influential Catholic writer of our time, expressed in print his disappointment with the church-as-institution, with its bishops, and with the pope.

Thomas Merton, the famous Trappist monk and author, complained in letters and in his private journals about certain church leaders and about some of those in authority in the religious order he belonged to.

Many Catholic women are angry with the church of our time for what they see as its intransigence on issues such as the ordination of women to the priesthood, sexist liturgical language and images, and women's nonpresence, in general, in church leadership roles.

Still, Romano Guardini remained a Catholic and a priest, Thomas Merton remained a Catholic and a Trappist monk, and Andrew Greeley remains a Catholic and a priest in good standing. Some women leave the church, but many more stay. Countless ordinary Catholics who object, for example, to the church's official teaching on birth control, or who were at one time hurt by an insensitive or ignorant priest, cherish their faith and remain in the church.

Such people understand that institution and tradition cannot be separated. But they also realize that sometimes it's necessary to distinguish between the church-as-institution, on the one hand, and, on the other, the Catholic community and living Catholic tradition. Many Catholics disagree with the church's leaders on certain institutional issues and/or official teachings, but they remain Catholics, as Andrew Greeley's sociological research indicates, because they like being Catholics; they love the community and they love the living Catholic tradition.

True love means accepting the loved one along with his or her faults and failings. Many Catholics reject certain secondary or non-essential aspects of Catholicism but remain in the church because they realize that to walk away would be to abandon a source of life and meaning that they would be hard-pressed to match anyplace else.

Years ago, Father Andrew Greeley put it this way: If you can find a perfect church go ahead and join it, but as soon as you do it won't be perfect anymore.

It isn't just in the church that I have had to confront imperfection, even evil, and respond to it. I have had to cope with inexplicable darkness caused by the choices others have made, choices I had no control over. Only the faith I first experienced and learned about in a Catholic school enables me to face this darkness and to believe that the light in my life, not the darkness, is the key to life's true meaning.

On June 19, 1988, near his northern California home, my father took his own life. It was Father's Day.

That morning, Dad insisted that he and my stepmother go to breakfast at a restaurant that had once been their favorite Sunday-morning spot. Later, back in his living room, he chatted by phone with my sister, who called to wish him a happy Father's Day.

A while after lunch, my stepmother noticed Dad was gone. She assumed he had wandered over to see friends who lived nearby. In fact, he had put a loaded handgun in his jacket pocket and set out walking in the warm afternoon sun. He hiked a couple of miles until he reached a two-lane highway, which he followed along the side of the road.

For some reason, a sheriff's deputy had stopped his squad car off the pavement. Dad approached the deputy standing outside the vehicle, took his wallet out of his rear pants pocket and held it out for the officer to take. "Here," he said, "I want you to have this. I'm going to kill myself." Those were his last words.

As my father turned and began to walk away, the officer called out, "Hey! Wait!" At that, Dad turned and pointed his gun at the deputy, who froze.

Walking on a little further, Dad lowered his small frame—at sixty-five he stood five feet seven inches and weighed, at most,

145 pounds—to a sitting position at the side of the road, his back to the deputy. He raised the handgun to his head and, in the words of the brief newspaper account the next day, "fired one round."

At that precise moment, I was driving with my wife and three young sons over Snoqualmie Pass, making the five-hour return trip from Seattle to our home on the eastern side of the state. Two days earlier, we had driven over to watch the Mariners go down in glorious defeat to the Oakland A's. Our three sons had been thrilled to see Jose Canseco and Mark McGwire in the flesh.

As we cruised along I-90, it occurred to me that I had forgotten to send a Father's Day card and I remarked on the oversight to my wife. I decided I'd phone Dad as soon as we got home.

My mind drifted to a birthday card I'd sent him the previous April: On the front was a drawing of a goofy dog and under it, "In honor of your birthday, my champion stunt dog Rex will tap out your age with his paws." On the inside of the card, Rex tapped like mad, and tapped some more, until finally he lay there dead with x's for eyes. "Hey!" said the final caption. "You killed my dog!"

Within minutes after we got home the phone rang. It was my mother. She took a deep breath, then told me that she had just had a call from my sister. My father had shot himself. Shocked, I said, "Are you kidding?" Right away, I wondered why I said that. She wouldn't kid about my father shooting himself. She told me what she knew, which wasn't much, and that was that.

I have few memories of my father being around home when I was a boy. He worked in the logging industry and often seemed to be gone. The summers when I was between ten and fourteen years old, Dad paid me a few dollars a day to help him survey timber land. Usually those days in the hot, dusty mountains included him telling me vulgar jokes, which embarrassed me intensely. Almost always, he also would end up redfaced with anger, swearing at me for not completing some task to his satisfaction.

One day when I was about fourteen, Dad towed a classic old auto into our garage—a 1927 Durant, as I recall. It was in bad shape, rusted all over, but it could be rescued. "We'll restore it," he said, and he showed me how to sand the rusty body by hand. We worked together for maybe ten minutes, then he went in the house and left me to work alone. He never returned to this project, but he often admonished me to get on out there and keep sanding. I soon gave it up too.

When I was fifteen, with no warning, Dad left my mother, my sister and me, moved to California, and did not show up again until my high school graduation almost three years later. Mom had to sell our house and move us into a little one-bedroom apartment in an old four-story brick building where my bed folded down out of a closet in the tiny living room. Dad sent token child-support checks at irregular intervals, and Mom eventually found a minimum-wage job in a small drugstore.

My father coped with his personal demons by drinking, sometimes heavily. Once, when I was about twelve, he remarked to me that I would understand when I grew up. When he was drinking he sometimes made a weird, high-pitched noise that frightened me. On a few occasions, my friends witnessed him "stewed to the gills" (the phrase was his) and I felt like crawling under the nearest rock.

I try to understand him. Though he was a poor excuse for a father, I don't doubt that he did the best he could, according to his lights; apart from spankings when I was little, he never resorted to physical abuse.

His own father died when Dad was quite young, maybe seven years old. He didn't try to educate himself by reading, and in spite of the fact that the whole family joined the Catholic Church when my sister and I were young, he was not a religious person.

In the weeks that followed Dad's suicide, rarely a day went by that I did not think about what he'd done. I tried to reconstruct the circumstances of his death in my imagination. I insisted that my stepmother send me the newspaper clipping that described how he killed himself. I wanted to know as much as I could. Why had he done it?

He had been afflicted with poor health for years as a result of a gunshot wound in his throat. Back in the early 1970s, while Dad was sitting in a car in a supermarket parking lot, a man walked up and fired a pistol point-blank for no apparent reason. Dad was running a lucrative bail-bond business at the time, so it's possible that his contacts with the seedier side of society had something to do with it. It was amazing that he survived at all, and it took pioneering surgery to repair his vocal chords so he could talk again.

About two weeks before Dad's suicide, a doctor told him there was no more they could do for his throat. Scar tissue continued to build up, and he was having difficulty breathing. He had suffered a heart attack six months earlier, and surgery to remove the scar tissue was considered too great a risk.

It is likely that Dad's suicide was a simple case of a guy who figured that his life was over anyway. Depressed, he saw no reason to wait around to die slowly and painfully by suffocation.

I still ponder the fact that Dad killed himself so matter-of-factly, as if he were going out to get a loaf of bread. It was all neatly planned and carried out, with no loose ends. *Here's my wallet, so you'll know who I am and who to inform.*

Did he give any thought to the effect his suicide would have on other people? Maybe, but he probably concluded that it couldn't be helped. Did he think of his suicide as an act of courage? Knowing him, I find that possible; he faced life with a kind of pathetic, juvenile bravado, and when he decided to do something he didn't care if others thought it was stupid. This is what he meant by courage.

So he left no note, made no final symbolic gesture; he simply decided to kill himself, and then he did. Bang. I can easily imagine him saying, "So what? It's nobody else's damn business."

I am a contented, happily married person who enjoys life, and I love and enjoy my children. I enjoy my work. I think, however, that I am happy in great part because of my determination not to be the kind of husband and father Dad was. I suppose he did me a perverse favor by showing me how not to do it.

I'm not the perfect father myself: I'm too authoritarian and I yell at my kids too much. But I do good things, too. When Kathy and I first became parents, we decided to arrange our work schedules so I could be home at least half of each workday. I've changed more diapers and read more bedtime stories than you can shake a stick at. When I tuck our boys into bed, I never fail to tell each one that I love him. I give hugs in abundance, I help with homework, I praise the latest achievement in spelling bee or band. Although I'm no big sports fan, I find myself enthusiastic about baseball; at every opportunity I take the boys to the minor league games in the city where we live.

One of the big questions in my mind is whether or not my father specifically chose Father's Day to kill himself. He was aware of what day it was. Could it be that he chose that day purposely so his children would not forget him? If so, it was the only time I know of that he ever came close to admitting that he, too, needed to be loved.

I feel pity for my father more than anything else. In spite of the many frustrations of family life, there is nothing that gives my life more meaning than loving my wife and sharing life with our children, watching them grow. If my father had

known this same kind of meaning in his life, perhaps he would
have longed to go on living and would have been willing to let
death bide its time in spite of the pain.

Perhaps my father would not have been so ready to walk
away from home on a warm Father's Day afternoon and put a
bullet in his brain.

I suppose I'll live with the questions for the rest of my life,
but there is one thing I am sure of. I learned as a child in a
Catholic school that suicide was an unforgivable sin, certain to
send a person straight to eternal agony in hell. On the contrary,
along with contemporary church teachings and moral theology, I no longer believe in a God who would do such a thing.
My father fell from overwhelming loneliness into God's tender
mercies.

As I reflected on my father's death in the first weeks after
his suicide, from some place in my unconscious, I suppose,
came the words of a prayer I had memorized so many years
before as a Catholic school kid. The prayer I remembered was
"An Act of Hope":

> O my God, relying on Thy almighty power and infi-
> nite mercy and promises, I hope to obtain pardon of
> my sins, the help of Thy grace, and life everlasting,
> through the merits of Jesus Christ, my Lord and
> Redeemer.

I prayed these words for my father and for myself.

Ultimately, my father's suicide raised for me in a personal
way the problem of death. Death had never struck so close to
home before. But the more I reflected on my father's death,
and on death in general, I realized that yes, death must come as
a shock. But my faith—that is, the ongoing experience of loving intimacy with the risen Christ as a member of the Catholic
community—has brought me to a place where death no longer
seems like such a big deal.

The prospect of my own death is a fearful one, but, on the
other hand, Jesus died to show us how to accept death. Un-

doubtedly, what I will find on the other side of death will be the biggest surprise I have ever had. But the surprise, I believe, will be in how great the loving acceptance and welcome will be that I find there.

In the late nineteenth century, in one of his letters to his brother, Theo, Vincent van Gogh wrote:

> Just as we take the train to get to Tarascon or Rouen, we take death to reach a star. . . .
>
> So it seems possible that cholera, gravel, tuberculosis and cancer are the celestial means of locomotion, just as steamboats, buses and railways are the terrestrial means. To die quietly of old age would be to go there on foot.

Before death, of course, life includes anguish, pain, and suffering, along with joy, peace, and fulfillment. As a Catholic school kid in the 1950s, I learned that even suffering can have a positive purpose. If something unpleasant happened to us, Sister Angelica's advice was to "offer it up."

We could benefit in the long run by uniting, in a kind of mystical fashion, our small suffering with the great suffering of Christ on the cross. Not that there was anything lacking in the sacrifice of love offered on our behalf by the Son of God, but we could still offer our suffering as a prayer for the good of others, in this world and the next.

This explanation satisfied me through high school, but later as I got into my theological studies in college, it became less satisfying, at least intellectually. Why do innocent children suffer and die? I wondered. Not an original question, but now I asked it. Why do so many good people suffer from injustice, or seem to just get by, while people who do bad things lounge around in Fat City?

Eventually, I found myself steeped in the Book of Job, which I now believe offers the best response to such questions, although even Job has its limits.

Sooner or later, at one time or another, on our own behalf or on behalf of others, we find it easy to share Job's words: "I loathe my life; I will give free utterance to my complaint; I will speak in the bitterness of my soul. I will say to God, Do not condemn me; let me know why you contend against me. Does it seem good to you to oppress, to despise the work of your hands and favor the schemes of the wicked? . . . Your hands fashioned and made me; and now you turn and destroy me. Remember that you fashioned me like clay; and will you turn me to dust again?" (10:1–3, 8–9).

The Lord answers Job "out of the whirlwind" (38:1), sarcasm in his voice: "Who is this that darkens counsel by words without knowledge?" (38:2). The Lord puts Job in his place saying, in effect, How can you with your puny brain hope to understand the mystery of suffering? Don't be so arrogant as to think you can penetrate this mystery; only believe that in the divine scheme, suffering has a place, unacceptable though it seems to you.

"Where were you when I laid the foundation of the earth? Tell me, if you have understanding. Who determined its measurements—surely you know! Or who stretched the line upon it? On what were its bases sunk or who laid its cornerstone when the morning stars sang together and all the heavenly beings shouted for joy?" (38:4–7).

When I first pondered these lines from Job, it struck me that not only does the Lord tell Job to put up or shut up. The Lord also says that when he created the world and human existence the way it is—including suffering and death—all of it was so spectacularly good that "the morning stars sang together and all the heavenly beings shouted for joy."

Suffering and death, even sometimes in the lives of little children, seem to be completely unjust, completely intolerable. Knowing this, Jesus accepted the anguish and pain of a totally unjust torture and death, to show us that in spite of appearances, these things have their place. By his example, Jesus urges us to trust, in our loving intimacy with him, that this is so; he urges us to trust that on the other side of suffering and death the morning stars sing together and all the heavenly beings shout for joy.

Ten

Jesus Is with Us

The first time I walked through the doors of Saints Peter and Paul School, the August before I entered third grade, the first thing I saw was a large plaster statue of Jesus standing on a pedestal, facing me some fifteen feet away. The statue was about half life-size, much larger than your typical tabletop religious statue.

The plaster Jesus wasn't much bigger than I was, and he had his arms raised in blessing, palms outward, so you could see precise little red wounds in his hands. On the statue's chest, outside his robes, his Sacred Heart stood out amidst golden rays and a crown of thorns. Jesus was barefoot, so you could see tidy little red wounds in his feet, as well. His shoulder-length plaster hair was painted brown, as were his eyes, and Jesus' skin was pale except for the subtle blush in his cheeks.

The statue of Jesus impressed me, especially his face, which seemed at the same time kind and sad. It wasn't great art, to be sure; it wasn't Michelangelo's Pieta, but I liked it.

One day, something happened. A boy threw a football in the school hallway, which was forbidden, and the ball hit the statue of Jesus and knocked his left arm almost completely off. The painted plaster arm was attached at the shoulder, and I have a picture in my mind of Sister Angelica the next day raising her arms, gently placing her hands under Jesus' arm, testing to see if it was firmly in place again.

The first image of Jesus I ever had came, I think, from that colorful plaster statue that stood in the hallway of the first Catholic school I attended. But I gained other images of Jesus soon. The small crucifix that hung above the chalkboard in our classroom presented a different image of Jesus. It occurred to me one day that the crucifix was "before," and the statue was "after." From this I got the rather sophisticated notion that the dead Jesus on the crucifix wasn't the last word; the statue Jesus out in the hall was how the story ended. Resurrection followed death.

A particular prayer touched me early in life. Sister Angelica handed out holy cards regularly, and one had a traditional prayer called the "Anima Christi" ("Soul of Christ") on the back. This prayer and the crucifix became united in my imagination to make the crucifix, for me, an image of great love:

> Soul of Christ, sanctify me;
> Body of Christ, save me;
> Blood of Christ, inebriate me;
> Water from the side of Christ, wash me;
> Passion of Christ, strengthen me.
> O good Jesus, hear me;
> Within your wounds hide me;
> Never permit me to be separated from you;
> From the wicked enemy defend me;
> In the hour of my death call to me
> And bid me come to your side,
> That with your saints I may praise you,
> For ever and ever. Amen.

One line, in particular, grabbed my attention: "Blood of Christ, inebriate me. . . ." I was asking God to let the blood of his Son make me drunk! What a graphic image! Sister said it meant that we want God to make us so happy and joyful in our faith that getting drunk from drinking beer or wine would pale by comparison.

Years later, I discovered that great line in the Acts of the Apostles. On Pentecost, the disciples gather and, "All of them were filled with the Holy Spirit and began to speak in other languages, as the Spirit gave them ability" (2:4). Some of the onlookers say, "They are filled with new wine" (2:13).

Even as a young boy, I gathered that faith must be something else again if it could make you feel like you were on a toot!

There were other images of Jesus, of course, all of them visual. Stained glass windows in churches portrayed a Jesus who carried a lamb on his shoulders, and a Jesus who sat behind a long table with his apostles at the Last Supper. One of the classrooms in the school had a toddler Jesus with an ornate crown on his head, wearing the lacy, gold-embroidered gowns an old-fashioned child king might wear. Someone explained that this statue was called the Infant of Prague. I had no idea what or where Prague was.

Every Christmas, both in church and at home a manger scene appeared with baby Jesus the center of attention. Mary and Joseph hovered over the manger, the shepherds and the Wise Men close by. The manger scene my grandparents set up on the mantle over their fireplace even had an angel above the stable holding a scroll-like sign that said, "Gloria in Excelsis Deo."

In later years, when I became a father, I thought, hmm, how appropriate and how wonderfully human. A similar thought filled my heart each of the three times a child was born to us: Glory to God in the highest. Subsequently, when a crying baby kept us awake at night, or a storming teenager made us doubt our sanity at having children in the first place, I had less inspiring thoughts.

Jesus had been a baby, just like me and just like anybody who ever lived. I looked closely at the infant Jesus in the manger scene in church, and sure enough . . . he had a belly button. That cinched it for me. People said Jesus was God, but if he had a belly button that made him just as human as I was.

From my childhood, my images of Jesus were varied, and these images shaped my thoughts and feelings about Jesus. At the same time, the *Baltimore Catechism* walked the straight and narrow. The Jesus I learned about from the old catechism was an abstraction. The answers to Questions 78 through 104 declared in no uncertain terms that Jesus is "the Saviour of all men," that he is "God made man," and that he is God because "He is the only Son of God, having the same divine nature as His Father."

The catechism insisted that Jesus is "man" because "He is the Son of the Blessed Virgin Mary and has a body and soul like ours."

So far, so good. But at this point, for me the discussion began to slip into a theological Twilight Zone, if there had been such a thing in the 1950s.

The catechism went to some length to deny things I had no wish to promote. It was heresy "to say that there are two Persons in Christ." On the other hand, it was okay to say that Jesus "has two natures: the nature of God and the nature of man." I was in the third grade! What *was* this?!

Was Jesus always "man"? the catechism asked. Slipping into a rare lower-case usage—on second thought, it was probably a typographical error—the catechism responded that, "The son of God was not always a man, but became man at the time of the Incarnation." "Incarnation"? No problem, the next question and answer were at the ready: "By the Incarnation is meant that the Son of God, retaining His divine nature, took to Himself a human nature, that is, a body and soul like ours."

The catechism went on to instruct me in further facts. The Son of God was "made man" when he was "conceived and made man by the power of the Holy Ghost in the womb of the Blessed Virgin Mary." Friendly reader, in the third grade "womb" meant nothing, n-o-t-h-i-n-g, to me. I used this word all the time when praying the Hail Mary ("the fruit of thy womb, Jesus"), and it meant zero.

One day I asked my mother why the nuns didn't have any children, and she replied, "Because they aren't married." This reply satisfied my curiosity, which ought to say something about not telling kids more about sex than they are ready and willing to hear.

Question 87: "When was the Son of God conceived and made man?" Answer: "The Son of God was conceived and made man on Annunciation Day, the day on which the Angel Gabriel announced to the Blessed Virgin Mary that she was to be the Mother of God."

I had visions of the Angel Gabriel looking at his celestial calendar: "Whoops! It's Annunciation Day! I almost missed it! Good thing I looked at my calendar! I gotta get down there and deliver that announcement to the Blessed Virgin Mary!"

NOT!

The *Baltimore Catechism* had the same perspective on all the important dates. It was as if they were named well in advance of the events themselves. "When was Christ born?"

Answer: "Christ was born of the Blessed Virgin Mary on Christmas Day in Bethlehem, more than nineteen hundred years ago." "When did Christ die?" Answer: "Christ died on Good Friday." "When did Christ rise from the dead?" Answer: "Christ rose from the dead, glorious and immortal, on Easter Sunday, the third day after his death."

The catechism insisted that the Son of God was both "God and man," but it clearly emphasized the divine side of the equation; Jesus was God, which made him seem distant, removed from my world and my experience. Even the historical events surrounding Christ's death and resurrection had a heavenly, ahistorical, fantastic ring to them. "Where," for example, "was Christ's body while His soul was in limbo?" Answer: "While His soul was in limbo, Christ's body was in the holy sepulchre." Not in a tomb or grave, mind you, but in "the holy sepulchre."

In a fine bit of theological extrapolation since found wanting, the old catechism explained that when the Apostles' Creed said that Christ "descended into hell," this meant that he "descended into a place or state of rest, called limbo, where the souls of the just were waiting for Him."

The Apostles' Creed simply means to emphasize that Jesus really did die, it wasn't an act of divine *leger demain*.

The catechism insisted that the reason Christ rose from the dead to was to prove something: "to show that he is true God. . . ."

Over and over, the catechism emphasized the divinity of Christ, never referring to him as "Jesus," a further way to downplay his humanity. Christ "as God is equal to the Father, and . . . as man He shares above all the saints in the glory of his Father and exercises for all eternity the supreme authority of a king over all creatures."

Question 104 delivered the ultimate statement on who Christ is: "What do we mean when we say [in the Apostles' Creed] that Christ will come from thence to judge the living and the dead?" Answer: "[We] mean that on the last day Our Lord will come to pronounce a sentence of eternal reward or of eternal punishment on everyone who has ever lived in this world."

Oh, wow. It's a good thing there was more to what I learned in the Catholic schools of the 1950s than what was in the *Baltimore Catechism*. The catechism had its impact, but when push came to shove, the statues, stained glass windows, other religious art, the Christmas story, and traditional prayers touched me on a deeper level.

The strongest images of Jesus that I carried around, in my heart if not my head, were not the daunting abstractions in the catechism but the warm, intriguing—admittedly sometimes sappy—images I found in the statue of the Sacred Heart, the stained glass Good Shepherd and Jesus of the Last Supper, the crowned and curiously costumed Infant of Prague, the baby Jesus in the manger, and the "Anima Christi."

In high school, four years of religion classes didn't alter my images of Jesus. We no longer used the *Baltimore Catechism*, but the books we did use, which I don't remember at all, did not raise the question of who Jesus was. That issue had been settled years ago for any kid who attended a Catholic elementary school. With the one-sided "Jesus is God" catechism theology behind me—though still active in my intellect—statues, stained glass windows, and the Christmas story continued to shape my feelings and imagination during my Catholic high school years.

In my junior year in high school, during a school retreat, I first came across Cardinal John Henry Newman's famous prayer-poem for a holy death:

> May the Lord support us
> all the day long,
> till the shades lengthen
> and the evening comes
> and the busy world is hushed,
> and the fever of life is over,
> and our work is done.
>
> Then in his mercy may he give us a safe lodging
> and a holy rest,
> and peace at the last.
>
> Amen.

I took Newman's great poetry as a prayer to Christ. It suggested images of a caring, compassionate Lord. As the years passed, the world indeed became a busy place, life often fevered and filled with work, and Newman's prayer carries deeper meaning for me the older I get. I have more appreciation now than when I was seventeen years old for the idea of "a safe lodging / and a holy rest, / and peace at the last."

During my four years in the U.S. Navy, my images of Jesus remained unchanged. On a cognitive level, I retained the Christ of the *Baltimore Catechism,* a God-man who was mostly God, only incidentally man. My mind affected my emotions, of course, especially when I confessed my sins to a priest in one of the old-style confessional booths. Then the God-man was a severe and demanding judge who could and definitely would send me to hell for all eternity if I missed Mass on Sunday just once. No ifs, ands, or buts about it. The Christ of the confessional was severe and terrifying.

On the other hand, this same Christ freely forgave me all my sins, and to receive absolution from a priest brought a feeling of relief and liberation that swept over me like a cool, comforting breeze on a hot, humid summer day. If confessing my sins was hell, receiving absolution was the sheerest heaven.

On an emotional level, most of the time during my Navy years I clung to the human Jesus of the stained glass windows, the crucifix, the old prayers, the statues, and the Christmas story. I related on an emotional level to a Jesus who cared about me personally and was with me all the time, ready to listen and guide.

During my second year in Hawaii, I was stationed at the U.S. Naval Air Station at Barber's Point, and I decided to attend Mass every day that I could. Most days, the priest and I were the only ones present. He was an older man, a lieutenant commander with a full head of snow-white hair who had spent almost his entire priesthood as a Navy chaplain. He was, I heard, an alcoholic, and his flushed face and the network of visible tiny blood veins in his nose showed it. He was a kindly man, and I think he appreciated having someone show up for daily Mass.

The old chaplain never gave a homily at weekday Masses, but one day he made an exception. He preached for five minutes to me, a congregation of one, and the subject of his sermon was Jesus. I don't remember most of what he said, but for some reason I do recall his concluding words. He said something like this: "Jesus is God, but he is most God when he is most human. Therefore, we become most God-like the more human we become and the more willingly we carry the crosses life sends our way."

Eighteen months later, I was a student at a Catholic university in California, eventually a Religious Studies major, and before long I began to understand what the old priest had said one sunny day in Hawaii. I began to understand how important it is to take the humanity of Jesus seriously. Jesus became a human being to show us how to be human ourselves. Therefore, unless we take his humanity seriously we devalue our own humanity, and to do that is to mock the God who created us.

As with my understanding of other aspects of the Catholic-Christian life, my biblical studies had a tremendous impact on my understanding of who and what Jesus is; the scripture scholars and theologians call it "Christology."

My Christology had been heavily weighted by the *Baltimore Catechism* in favor of a God-man whose humanity it was important to affirm for doctrinal reasons. But in everyday, practical spiritual terms, his humanity was not terribly important. Now I began to discover that just the opposite was true. Had it not been for the human Jesus I found in statues, stained glass windows, prayers, and the Christmas story, my spirituality would have been un-Christian in the extreme.

Plowing into my New Testament studies, I discovered how important Jesus' humanity is to all the documents I found there. Each of the Gospels has a unique way to emphasize how human Jesus was. Matthew and Luke, for example, the only two Gospels that have infancy narratives, include those stories in part to insist that Jesus had a human mother, that he slipped into the world from between the legs of a young woman, and received nourishment from her breasts, full with milk, at a particular point in human history. If this shocks us, then our grasp of the Incarnation is naive, at best.

I learned that one primary purpose of Matthew's lengthy genealogy of Jesus (1:2–16) is to highlight Jesus' place in a human family line, albeit the royal line of King David.

Matthew also locates Jesus' birth in a "house" (2:11), the most ordinary of locations, thus emphasizing how human Jesus' circumstances were from the beginning of his human life.

"While they were there [in Bethlehem]," Luke's Gospel says, "the time came for her to deliver her child. And she gave birth to her firstborn son. . . ." (2:6). Thus, Luke makes even more explicit the humanity of Jesus than does Matthew. Luke alone gives us the very human story of Jesus at age twelve, left behind in the temple where Mary and Joseph find him later, "sitting among the teachers, listening to them and asking them questions" (2:46).

As a college student, I was amazed and delighted to discover that Mark, the earliest Gospel, frequently illustrates Jesus' humanity by describing his emotions. When a leper begs Jesus to cure him, Jesus is "moved with pity" (1:41).

Mark says that when Jesus returned to Nazareth, "his hometown," and taught in the synagogue, "he was amazed at their unbelief" (6:2, 6).

Upon seeing the "great crowd" that came to hear him teach, Jesus "had compassion for them, for they were like sheep without a shepherd. . . ." (6:34).

When the Pharisees argue with Jesus and insist that he prove who he is by giving them "a sign from heaven," Jesus "sighed deeply from his spirit" (8:12), an expression of weariness and frustration.

A wealthy man asks Jesus what he must do to gain eternal life, and when the man exhibits sincere dedication to his religious tradition, Mark says that "Jesus, looking at him, loved him. . . ." (10:21).

I was impressed by how graphically Mark portrayed Jesus' humanity in his account of the suffering and death of Jesus. Mark says that in the Garden of Gethsemane Jesus was "distressed and agitated" (14:33). Jesus says to his disciples, "I am deeply grieved, even to death. . . ." (14:34).

Scandalous though it may seem, Mark reports that Jesus' last words from the cross were words of despair: "My God, my God, why have you forsaken me?" (15:34). How else are we to interpret this? As he died, Jesus spoke words that came from the depth of his humanity at his darkest moment, simply that and nothing more. His cry of despair expressed his feelings, but they were not an act of the will. Mark wants us to know that Jesus experienced the full range of human feelings and emotions, just as we do.

We may think that it would be more inspiring if Jesus' last words, in the midst of an agonizingly slow death, had been an expression of faith and trust in his Father, but Mark says that this was not the case. Mark was determined to let Jesus' humanity show in all its truth and depth, thereby teaching us that God doesn't abandon us even when our feelings are feelings of despair. It was how Jesus had lived his life that mattered; and it was how he began his agony, abandoning himself to the will of his Father, that mattered: "Abba, Father . . . not what I want, but what you want" (14:36).

So important is it that we take Jesus' humanity seriously, I learned, that even John's Gospel, which highlights Jesus' divinity more than any of the other Gospels, insists over and over that Jesus was human right down to his toes. Following a long ode to the Divine Word, John states flatly that "the Word became flesh and lived among us" (1:14).

The Jesus of the Fourth Gospel often seems to be the already risen Christ. Even during his passion and death, he is in control of the situation. "You would have no power over me," John's Jesus says to Pilate, "unless it had been given you from above. . . ." (19:11). When Peter cuts off the ear of the high priest's slave, Malchus, Jesus admonishes him: "Put your sword back into its sheath. Am I not to drink the cup that the Father has given me?" (18:11).

In John's Gospel, Jesus' last words are those of one who completed an assigned mission; there is no sign of despair or lack of control, as in Mark; Jesus dies when he is ready to die: "When Jesus had received the wine, he said, 'It is finished.' Then he bowed his head and gave up his spirit" (19:30).

Still, John's Jesus is completely human, too. In the account of the raising of Lazarus from the dead, found only in John,

Jesus' human emotions are on display. "When Jesus saw [Mary] weeping, and the Jews who came with her also weeping, he was greatly disturbed in spirit and deeply moved," John says (11:33). And, "Jesus began to weep" (11:35). When Jesus arrives at Lazarus' tomb, he is "again greatly disturbed" (11:38).

The Jesus of the Fourth Gospel reveals his divine nature explicitly. All the same, only a thoroughly human Messiah would say from the cross, "I am thirsty" (19:28).

Taken as a complete collection of theological statements, the documents of the New Testament place equal value and equal emphasis on both the humanity and divinity of Jesus the Christ. In the course of my undergraduate and graduate theological studies, I learned that the minute we begin to downplay one in favor of the other, or emphasize one at the cost of the other, we're in for trouble.

One of the most helpful books I read in recent years about Christology is *Models of Jesus,* by John F. O'Grady. Father O'Grady wrote that, "No one image [of Jesus] can be thought to be the exclusive portrayal of the meaning of the Lord, but each one does contribute to an overall picture."

When I taught an introductory course on the New Testament to undergraduates, I used the example of no less a personage than the late rock 'n' roll singer, Elvis Presley, who flushed his life away on drugs, booze, and fast living at the age of forty-two. No, I haven't seen him in a supermarket or in line at a movie theater. Actually, the example I used was the larger-than-life statue of Presley that stands in a prominent place before an important government building in Memphis, Tennessee.

The bronze statue of Elvis does not look like the late singer ever looked at any one point in his life. It has heroic dimensions and blends several Elvises into one image. The figure is dressed something like Elvis dressed when he entertained during the 1970s. His shirt is fringed buckskin, similar to but not exactly like shirts he wore in a couple of the B-grade movies he

appeared in during the '60s. Yet the shirt has a high collar like
the collars on the bejeweled, bell-bottom jumpsuits Elvis per-
formed in during the '70s. The statue's head looks like the
Elvis of the '60s, but he carries a guitar of the model he used
in the '50s.

Is this a statue of Elvis Presley? Absolutely. Does it look
like Elvis ever looked? Yes and no. It is one sculptor's image
of the late singer; it is an image that says more about the
artist's image of Elvis than it does about Elvis himself; it says
as much about the feelings of Elvis fans as it does about Elvis
Presley. Still, the sculptor's image definitely presents the actual
Elvis Presley who lived and breathed and recorded timeless
wonders such as "You Ain't Nothin' But a Hound Dog" and
one in which he went on about "a hunka hunka burnin'
love."

The artist who sculpted the bronze statue of Elvis Presley
that stands majestically before an important government
building in Memphis, Tennessee, is not unlike the authors of
the Gospels of Matthew, Mark, Luke, and John . . . no disrespect intended, I swear.

The sculptor of the Elvis statue worked with historical
information about Presley, but when it came to what the statue
would actually look like, the artist also relied upon his own
feelings and the emotions of Elvis fans after the singer's death
from drug abuse. The statue reflects not only the historical
Elvis but his fans' continued devotion to him and his music
after his body was socked away in an elaborate tomb on the
grounds of his mansion abode, Graceland.

After the death and resurrection of Jesus, no one fashioned
a bronze statue of him. But unique written documents developed, Gospels, and four of them were gradually accepted as
part of the sacred writings of the Christian community, the New
Testament. Each of the authors of the four Gospels worked
with historical information about Jesus, but each also had a
unique perspective on who Jesus was and his meaning for the
particular faith community he wrote his Gospel for. Each wrote

about Jesus in the light of his resurrection and the contemporary, ongoing experience of a particular faith community during the first century A.D.

Just as the statue of Elvis Presley is like yet unlike the historical Elvis, so each Gospel presents an image of Jesus that is both like and unlike the historical Jesus of Nazareth . . . again, no disrespect intended. The statue of Elvis Presley tells the truth about Elvis both historically and in terms of his continuing, probably romanticized, meaning for people after his demise.

In a similar but unique fashion, the Gospels present the truth about Jesus, each from a unique perspective, both historically and in terms of Jesus' meaning after his death and resurrection. In each Gospel we encounter not only the historical Jesus but the post-resurrection faith of the primitive church and the unique insights of those who actually wrote the Gospels. Each Gospel reflects not only the historical Jesus of Nazareth but the experience of a particular faith community's ongoing relationship with him.

If we could interview the person who sculpted the statue of Elvis, the artist would likely be able to explain the image or images of Elvis the statue is based upon. I had in mind, the sculptor might say, Elvis as a symbol of people's ability to overcome a past of poverty, obscurity, and ignorance to attain wealth and fame.

Just so, for example, the primary image of Jesus in the Gospel of Matthew is of Jesus as the New Moses. Writing for a predominantly Jewish Christian community, Matthew wanted to show that Jesus brought, and continues to bring, a way of life that both fulfilled and superseded the Mosaic Law. Thus, Matthew has Jesus ascend a mountain to deliver the New Law, the Sermon on the Mount, just as Moses ascended Mount Sinai and came back down with the Jewish Law. At the same time, Matthew didn't fabricate the Sermon on the Mount; it presents the actual teachings of Jesus of Nazareth, but interpreted in a way to make them fit the unique time and place of the faith community Matthew wrote his Gospel for in about 85 A.D.

Similar examples exist in just about every document in the New Testament; each presents a unique, slightly different image of Jesus, and each unique, slightly different literary image of Jesus is the inspired Word of God in human words.

As the years have gone by, since I first clapped eyes on the plaster statue of Jesus in a northern Idaho Catholic school, I have learned a few things about Jesus. I now know that in any culture where the Gospel has had an impact, each and every person, believer and nonbeliever alike, carries around a unique image, or sometimes set of images, of Jesus in his or her mind and imagination. My predominant image of Jesus is probably different from yours, and both of us have a different image of Jesus from other people we know.

It's also true that different Christian groups or communities have different images of Jesus. Fundamentalist Christians tend to have a "Personal Savior" image of Jesus. For them, the image of Jesus that believers should base their faith on is a personal savior you must invite into your life to rescue you from Satan and a sinful world. Their motto is, "Accept Jesus as your personal savior, and everything will be alright."

Even within a particular tradition, people have different images of Jesus. A very conservative Catholic's image of Jesus is likely to be considerably different from a very liberal Catholic's image of Jesus. Some people love the bestselling Joshua novels by Father Joseph Girzone, while the image of Jesus he presents there makes other people squirm. The image of Jesus cherished by Catholics in the Charismatic Renewal is different from the image of Jesus reflected in the work of liberation theologians and their disciples.

There is nothing wrong with a pluralism of images of Jesus. Each gives us a unique insight into the mystery of Jesus who was fully human and fully divine. The various images of Jesus I encountered early in life, as a Catholic school student, helped me throughout my life to be comfortable with many images of Jesus.

All this begs the question, What was Jesus really like? This question echoes one investigated by scripture scholars for

Everybody Has a Guardian Angel

many years, namely, what can we know about the actual, historical Jesus of Nazareth? The question and its various responses have a history that intrigued me in graduate school, but I won't bore you with that. Some years ago, scripture scholar Joseph A. Fitzmyer, S.J., wrote what I think is the best book on New Testament Christology in non-technical language: *A Christological Catechism: New Testament Answers.*

What can we know about the actual, historical Jesus of Nazareth? The question itself is complicated, because it is one that we ask that the authors of the New Testament had little interest in. Their dominant concern was the *meaning* of Jesus, not "historical facts."

Father Fitzmyer lays out, in a few paragraphs, the bare-bones information about Jesus that we can take as historical in the modern sense of the word, and it is singularly uninspiring. For example, Fitzmyer begins: "He was a Palestinian Jew born of a woman named Mary married to a carpenter, Joseph. He lived in Nazareth of Galilee. . . ."

The reader is likely to finish Fitzmyer's historical summary and respond with a big "ho-hum." And well we might, because it is not historical data about Jesus that matters, that makes a difference in people's lives. It is the living Jesus, risen and present among us who makes a difference, who transforms people, people's relationships, and people's outlook on life and the world. Our images of Jesus carry far more truth about Jesus than scientific historical research will ever turn up.

The images of Jesus I encountered in Catholic schools, from grade school through graduate school, help me to appreciate more deeply the mystery of the risen Jesus who is with us. To this day, among the words of Jesus I find to be the most comforting and the most challenging are the final words of the -risen Jesus to his disciples—meaning us, too—at the end of the Gospel of Matthew: "And remember, I am with you always, to the end of the age" (28:20).

Thank you, God our loving Father, for the gift of your Son, Jesus, who shows us how to live, and how to die, and shares with us even now the new life of his resurrection. Amen.